D1269186

Poems from Mandelstam

By the same author:

Poems from Mandelstam

Translated by R. H. Morrison

With an Introduction
by Ervin C. Brody

Rutherford ● Madison ● Teaneck
Fairleigh Dickinson University Press
London and Toronto: Associated University Presses

Associated University Presses
440 Forsgate Drive
Cranbury, NJ 08512

Associated University Presses
25 Sicilian Avenue
London WC1A 2QH, England

Associated University Presses
P.O. Box 488, Port Credit
Mississauga, Ontario
Canada L5G 4M2

Library of Congress Cataloging-in-Publication Data

Mandel'shtam, Osip, 1891–1938.
  [Poems. English. Selections]
  Poems from Mandelstam / translated by R.H. Morrison ; with an introduction by Ervin C. Brody.
    p.   cm.
  Includes bibliographical references.
  ISBN 0-8386-3382-X (alk. paper)
  I. Morrison, R. H. (Robert Hay), 1915–   .   II. Title.
PG3476.M335A26   1990
891.713—dc20   88-46184
                                                                          CIP

PRINTED IN THE UNITED STATES OF AMERICA

To my incomparable friend
Xenia Meissner

Poetry is the consciousness of one's rightness.

Osip Mandelstam

Contents

Preface

Writing in 1964 about the early years of the magazine *Novy Mir* (New world), N. Smirnov described how Osip Mandelstam had once reacted to a young poet who, in Mandelstam's opinion, had not shown him due deference. "You must not only listen to me, young man," he said, "but also pay heed to every word of mine, because every word of mine is for the history of literature." The remark is quoted in a context in which the author refers to Mandelstam as being extremely proud and suspicious and as sometimes displaying unpleasant arrogance. Perhaps so, but, some sixty years later, how right the poet's resounding prophecy has proved to be! In our time Mandelstam (1891–1938) has come into his own as one of the great poets of the twentieth century. He belongs not only to Russia, the country in which he lived and was persecuted and destroyed, but to the whole world; indeed, his very name having been officially obliterated in the USSR for some three decades after his death, he has belonged to us for much longer.

In 1967 the distinguished Mandelstam scholar Clarence Brown, of Princeton University, asked whether a true cult of Mandelstam, with its disadvantages, was coming into existence. No doubt it was, and still exists, just as there lingers a cult of Lorca, another poet-martyr of our time. But again, the lesser phenomenon fades beside the substantial reality of the poet's true stature. The more we know of Osip Mandelstam, the more he outgrows any limitations in earlier attitudes toward him.

The more we know of him, the more too we are struck by his many-sidedness and integrity. Mandelstam the poet is also Mandelstam the author of remarkable prose: there is no separation; one branch of his creative work is intertwined with another. His critical notes throw light on his poems; his poems echo his travel accounts. To appreciate him one must not be exclusive in one's reading. It is from his writings as a whole that we gain full appreciation of the breadth and depth of his learning and intuitions. A Christianized Jew born in Warsaw, he was perhaps the modern Russian poet most steeped in the majority of those various inheritances that have helped to make up European civiliza-

11

tion: the classical Greco-Roman, the Judaeo-Roman, Byzantium, the West, and Islam. "Child of Europe" was George Ivask's description of him.

Given the rare diversity and cohesion of Mandelstam's poetry and prose, there may be something invidious about a relatively small selection of translations from his poems alone. The time may still not yet have come, however, for some kind of Collected Works in English. It must be admitted that part of this poet's work is of lesser appeal also in the original and would have only academic, historical interest in translation. Mandelstam's greatest poems are much finer than some of his others—mere vignettes or ephemeral pieces. There seemed to be room, though, for a new selection in English, as a fair number of his poems appear to have been bypassed by most of the previous translators; certain other poems came to light too late to be considered for their selections. The following versions are drawn from all periods of Mandelstam's creative life of thirty years, some emphasis being placed on lesser-known pieces. At the same time, versions of a reasonable number of the finest, more famous lyrics have been included, simply because they could not have been left out. Even when several translators choose the same poems to translate and their resultant collections to some extent overlap, this is not strictly duplication: each translator in turn produces a *new* translation, a new interpretation, a new form of expression in the other language. A poet's translators are complementary, not competitive. No translation from Mandelstam is a poem by Mandelstam.

A translation from Mandelstam can do little more than suggest one aspect of the original. Osip Mandelstam, like Pushkin, created music in verse, architecture and sculpture in verse, and pictures in verse, as well as conveying other meanings in verse. He was one of modern Europe's most exquisitely melodious poets, akin in this respect to Verlaine. The music of poetry cannot be translated. True, Mandelstam, an excellent linguist, translated many poems into rhymed verse; but on the other hand one recalls the remark of his friend Anna Akhmatova to her friend Lydia Chukovskaya: "In one's own verses rhymes are wings, but in others', when one translates, they are a burden."

The following are prose translations in which an attempt has been made to present the *matter* of some of the poems; for the *manner* one must read the Russian. It is worth the effort, though it is well known that at times this poet's work can prove difficult, being condensed into a sort of poetic shorthand. It is in pondering the short cuts and allusions that a knowledge of the whole man is of particular help.

A prophecy, and allusions . . . Drawn as he was to Christian traditions, to Rome and Orthodoxy and their cathedrals and rites (see poems numbered 69, 84, 106, 117, 182), Mandelstam nevertheless retained characteristics of the Jewish prophets. His exclamations (27, 30, 162) and lamentations suggest those of the Old Testament; 457 (xvii) provides an early example. His sometimes visionary language can strike one with the force of something out of Revelation. As in the case of Rilke, his poems contain many Old and New Testament references. It is not a *slave woman* in line 2 of 223, as the Russian suggests, but "the handmaid of the Lord" (Luke 1:38).

Dualisms and contrasts abound in Mandelstam, giving tension and amplitude to his poetry: religion and philosophy; subjectivity and objectivity; sublime heights and everyday scenes of the streets of Leningrad and Moscow (142, 159). Many of his works have a twofold basis, physical and metaphysical; a pillar of Acmeism—a kind of Parnassianism—he was also a thoroughgoing Symbolist at times! The polarities in his thought enabled him at the age of nineteen to write the remarkable poem "Silentium" (14), in which he joins to the briefest outline of a Greek myth his vision of existence's flowing back into the formless void of Chaos—a Genesis in reverse. A lengthy essay could be written on the contrasts and seeming oppositions in Mandelstam: the "lonely" young man (22) was already blessed with many friends, and he was "not lonely in the prison of the world" (8); proud and independent, he became ever more dependent on the support of his heroic wife as ostracism and persecution increased; and so on. But Mandelstam's personality was essentially integrated, and in that lay much of his strength.

One last comment. The reader will notice the frequent repetition of favorite imagery. This is not a feature merely of this selection; it is part and parcel of Mandelstam. We have the swallow and the abyss, and transparency and the crystalline over and over again. The swallow and the abyss (113), like Hölderlin's eagles over the abyss, are a potent conjunction of archetypal images.

The versions in the following pages, and some references in this Preface, are based on the Russian four-volume edition of *Collected Works* edited by G. P. Struve and B. A. Filippov; vol. 4 co-edited by N. Struve (1–3, Washington and New York, Inter-Language Literary Associates, 1967–71; 4, Paris, YMCA-Press, 1981). This outstanding work of scholarship puts all readers and students of Mandelstam deeply in its debt. With revisions and addenda, it has grown with the years, keeping pace with, and playing a leading part in, the spread of the poet's fame in the English-speaking world, as elsewhere. Grateful acknowledgment is made to this Mandelstam treasure-house of texts, notes, reminiscences, and critical studies. The numbering of the translations follows that of the Russian originals, as does the authentic dating of the poems, or conjectural dating shown in square brackets by the Russian editors·mostly on the basis of the date of first publication. It should be noted, however, that, whereas poems taken from Nos. 1–395 are, at least within their sections, in chronological order, or supposed chronological order (1908–37), the group numbered 457 (twelve translated out of twenty-two), though placed toward the end, are early works dating from 1909 or 1910. Published in Paris in 1970, they are believed to have been drawn from previously unpublished letters of Mandelstam to Vyacheslav Ivanov. Most of these lyrics by the then pre-Acmeist poet aged eighteen or nineteen are quiet in tone, and some are reminiscent of the French Symbolists. At other times, in 457 (xv and xix), for instance, there is a hint of the mature Mandelstam who was soon to astonish hearers and readers with his originality, self-confidence, and courage, with a bold imagery and euphony given to few poets.

The epigraph of this book comes from Mandelstam's essay *On the Interlocutor*. The translation of these few words, incidentally, happens to be enough to illustrate the difficulty of rendering shades of meaning. The original sentence could be translated in scores of different ways, two of its main words, *soznanie* and *pravota*, each having many partial synonyms in both languages. Other versions might be: "Poetry is the acknowledgment of one's integrity," or "Poetry is the avowal of one's guiltlessness." Few poets can have understood these things better. Mandelstam could not shrink from knowledge and avowal of the truth. Mandelstam was right.

Acknowledgments

Some of these translations, as numbered below, appeared previously in the following magazines and newspaper: *The Southern Review* 8, 9, 175, 341, 352, 457 (xv); *Translation* 113, 116; *The Literary Review* 30, 66, 89, 145, 146, 150, 183, 223, 336, 354, 374; *The Antigonish Review* 106, 148, 162; *Quadrant* 14, 15, 30, 41, 65, 67, 69, 84, 113, 142, 148, 178, 182, 341, 457 (xii); *Overland* 13, 73, 163, 183, 374; *Redoubt* 8, 62, 155; *The Canberra Times* 6, 111; *The Phoenix Review* 11, 116.

Introduction

1

When Pushkin defied the Tsar with his youthful revolutionary poems and sided with his Decembrist friends in the ill-fated uprising in 1825, a literary-political tradition was born. In a country where the written word, and more broadly the creative arts, are a unique and mighty power, culture is a sort of magic that can cast spells. Thus, the imaginative writer has become accepted as a political spokesman with all the practical significance of that and hailed as the conscience of society in his fight for human rights.

The alienation of the disenchanted poet from his reading public and the identity crisis so frequent in Western societies never occurred in Russia. But he had to pay, especially in the Stalin period, curiously a time of explosive national creativity, a terrible price for his moral courage to confront the authorities. Praising "the beautiful and tragic production of the early years of the Russian Revolution," Albert Camus focused on the artist who previously used to sing "on the sidelines," while "in history's amphitheater" the lion devoured the martyr; now suddenly the artist finds himself thrown in the same amphitheater facing the lion. "This clearly illustrates [his] torment," says Camus, whose conclusion is that the artist must create at a "perpetual risk" since "the time of the irresponsible artist is over."[1] This was a fateful era in the history of the Soviet Union, a twilight of faith and hope, when the measure of decency was often the time spent in a jail or in exile. Addressing the precarious situation of poetry in his country, Alexander Blok, the great figure of Russia's Silver Age of poetry (end of the nineteenth and beginning of the twentieth century), wrote that "literature is a more vital force in Russia than anywhere else. Nowhere does Word become Life, nowhere does it turn into bread or stone as it does with us," adding that this is "perhaps why Russian writers die, come to grief, or simply fade away."[2]

Of course, not all Russian writers perished through violence. But many of the poets who survived the Russian Revolution—especially the four most important among them, Pasternak,

17

Akhmatova, Tsvetaeva, and Mandelstam—were subjected to the danger of prison and death by the conditions of history. In a certain sense all these poets, whose personal destinies were inextricably and fatally linked with the impersonal forces that tormented the country, were like one person sharing vital cultural traits, in some permanent way breathing together, feeling the same reactions, thinking each other's thoughts, strengthening each other's individuality and, while (in Akhmatova's phrase) "Russia, in her innocence, twisted in pain under blood-spattered boots," restoring some of their wounded identity.

Mandelstam himself had clearly anticipated his tragic destiny in those "terrible years"[3] of cultural genocide, for shortly after the revolution, infusing his art with personal history, he expressed, for the first time, the apprehension that was to haunt him all his life of "death as a penalty for poetic creation." This vatic poet once remarked that "only in Russia is poetry respected. It gets people killed. Where else is poetry so common a motive for murder?"[4] This prophecy about his bleeding poetry unfortunately proved true when he died in transit to one of Stalin's gulags on 28 December 1938. Today he is generally recognized as the greatest Russian poet of the twentieth century.

2

Born in Warsaw in 1891, Mandelstam grew up in a cultured Russian-Jewish family in Saint Petersburg. His parents provided an enlightened atmosphere for the young man that gave him a measure of emotional identity and security. After participating in the intellectual ferment of the well-known Tenishev private school, Mandelstam went to Paris, then to Heidelberg, where he studied Kant and Old French literature, and to Italy, where he became an admirer of Dante. These foreign visits triggered in him a lifelong devotion to European culture, languages, and classic literatures. "I received a blissful inheritance: / the wandering dreams of foreign singers" (67).[5]

Mandelstam took classes in philosophy, art, and history at the University of Saint Petersburg. All these varied interests are reflected in his early poetry. His poems began appearing in the *Apollon,* the best literary journal of the time, from 1908 on, and the startling originality of his first publication—a collection of lyrics under the title of *Stone* in 1913—gave him instant fame even in a country well-known for its fine poets.

Throughout his life Mandelstam led a kind of nomadic existence. During the First World War and the subsequent civil war he could still find some occasional work, but as the Bolshevik government consolidated itself, it became increasingly difficult for him to make a living. The civil war and its aftermath continued to inflict acute privations on most of the writers. Employment began to depend more and more upon one's being certifiably loyal to the new regime regardless of artistic skills. What the artist was asked, at the time, to embrace in the name of art was a specific politically-oriented attitude to life—an attitude totally alien to him. Mandelstam was thoroughly disliked by the authorities because of his independent voice and his unwillingness to take their side in the ideological struggle—conceived as the bulldozing of the poetic expressions of the past—that raged in literary circles during the 1920s. A poet is a rebel, and his song is "a form of linguistic disobedience." But it is a highly potent weapon because "its sound casts a doubt on more than a concrete political system: it questions the entire existential order."[6]

Poetry was the center of Mandelstam's life, and his own sense of importance to literature propelled him with the force of religious fervor to separate art from propaganda and rendered him immune to the shrill noises of the official manifestos. The age was lacking in soul behind its Potemkin village façade. Fulfilling a vital inner need, he tried to introduce into poetry a moral and ethical dimension that the authorities blotted out. It was at this time that his gradual fall from grace and subsequent harassment began to expose him fully to the storms and stresses of recurrent crises. His literary foes "politicized" his poetry, calling it subversive. As a result Mandelstam could publish less and less because the authorities warned editors of journals and publishing houses to be on guard against printing the work of a class enemy. As Brodsky indicates, "This contributed to Mandelstam's growing separation from any form of mass production. . . . the result was an effect in which the clearer the voice gets, the more dissonant it sounds . . . and the aesthetic isolation acquires physical dimensions."[7]

In 1922 he could still manage to publish a second book of poems called *Tristia* (the title was borrowed from Ovid), the central focus of which was supplied by the Russian Revolution. In history and literature a sense of injustice often combines with a messianic mission to speak out and communicate, whatever the cost. Carl Young once said that the function of an artist is to rectify the imbalance of a period in which he lives. The inner struggle between Mandelstam's sense of integrity and his feelings of despair and defeat now assumed almost cosmic dimensions. He was clearly heading toward an occupational suicide.

Thanks to the indomitable courage and writing skills of his widow, Nadezhda Mandelstam, whose main task in life was to hide

19

and to preserve for posterity the poetry and prose of her husband and to frustrate the efforts of the Soviet authorities to destroy all the evidence that her husband ever existed, the story of the poet's final years is now widely known through her two books of reminiscences: *Hope Against Hope* (1970) and *Hope Abandoned* (1974). Both titles are plays on Nadezhda Mandelstam's given name and the Russian word for hope. Memoirs of great passion and immediacy—indeed an illustration of what happens when the collective watches over the writer—they chronicle her husband's life under Stalin, telling of how this outwardly gentle poet of great intellectual honesty had to endure ignorance and hatred, how he was hounded, ostracized, exiled, and finally destroyed.

Mandelstam was first arrested in 1934 ostensibly for having written a bizarre poem in which he poked grim fun at Stalin, "the Kremlin mountaineer whose thick fingers squirm like worms" and whose "moustache laughs like a cockroach" and exposed the dictator's relish for torture and execution: "What is another killing to him?"[8]

He was expected to be shot, but a dramatic conversation between Stalin and Pasternak, and a timely intervention by Nikolai Bukharin, a prominent Bolshevik leader, who himself was later unjustly executed, saved him and instead he was exiled to the provincial town of Voronezh. Yet life became more and more hopeless for him. This was the time when Sergei Kirov, the Leningrad party chief, was assassinated—rumor has it on Stalin's orders—which then provided the pretext for the wholesale purges, show trials, and murders of the late 1930s.

The years of exile were a period of utter poverty, persecution, and illness that often drove the poet to the brink of insanity and suicide. It was a time when life was just barely possible and had to be lived at the outer edge of disaster. Yet, by a glaring artistic paradox, it was also a time of feverish poetic achievements, of late-blooming flowers as the poet tried to snatch a few precious moments of creative freedom from his existential inferno. The thrill of the spirit asserted itself in cathartic bursts of energy. The more brutal the oppression, the more painful the sense of loss and betrayal, the greater the literary space Mandelstam's productive talents conquered. Perhaps he hoped that this torrent of poetry might become, as it had during other critical periods of his life, a source of strength and revival. But worn out by physical infirmities and mental anguish, he could not create a lasting literary Maginot line of defense. His fate was inevitable. On 1 May 1938, he was arrested again, never to return. To this day the bulk of his poetry has not been published in the Soviet Union.

3

No Soviet poet of modern sensibility reflected so intensely as Mandelstam the loss of historical and philosophical self-assurance and the emerging discrepancies between state order and the isolation of individual consciousness. Several of his poems deal with the conflict between honor and obedience, the individual and the authorities, not unlike that felt by his heroine Antigone. He was chiefly concerned with the preservation of Russia's cultural and moral heritage, and his best poetry attests to the survival of art and conscience—for Mandelstam the two were inseparable—at a time and place when both seemed to have the flimsiest of chances to stay alive.

It is crucial to stress this particular aspect of Mandelstam's artistic life, since it would be impossible to grasp fully his poetry if it were considered in historical, political, and cultural isolation from the anxieties and sufferings that overwhelmingly dominated his mature existence. Every line and word are seen as a product of intention and choice. Thus, a critic has to approach Mandelstam as the poet was "inserting" (Camus's phrase) his poetry into his own time and trace the intricate personal and literary connections that bound him to such important historical events as the First World War, the Russian Revolution, the civil war, and, finally, the cataclysm of the Stalin terror that, as a climax, cost his life. In time Mandelstam acquired a sense of history that permitted him to convey not only the lyric moments of experience but the moral climate of the age, the quality of life of the fractured epoch, creating in this process a vast sociohistorical panorama. His life and art gave shape to the horrors of the time.

Yet he was no Solzhenitsyn to strike an ideological mortal blow at his enemies; his was, rather, a cry of nonideological anger against injustice. He avoided politics, but defied the official literary taste cultivated in the Soviet Union. He was a-Soviet rather than anti-Soviet. Believing that Stalinist history is not beyond criticism, he disdained to sanitize Soviet reality by editing out certain facts of life that some other poets, more in tune with the canons of socialist realism, preferred not to tackle. He refused to believe that socialist realism—"a truthful historically concrete depiction of reality in its revolutionary development" as it was officially declared and which Pasternak once described as masking "everything that is pompous, pretentious, rhetorical, without substance, useless in human terms and morally suspect"[9]—where art is made to serve extra-artistic purposes decided by the political leadership, where no other standard of taste, social or moral, was permitted to play any role in determining what sort of literature it

21

is appropriate for the government to support—was an absolute value. He felt that to deny the artist his freedom of expression to penetrate life's chaos and to make it meaningfully cohere amounted to cultural barbarism. He saw the dangers of this aesthetic policy in its attempt to drown the poet and his work in an ocean of political doctrine and historical interpretation. He was convinced that since literature, by its very nature, is often controversial, skeptical and disrespectful, it would be a travesty to sterilize it to make it more politically acceptable. The protracted and agonizing conflict between him and the Soviet literary establishment, the gap between his poetry and the officially sanctioned art was, in the words of a scholar, "less a deliberate resolve to mutiny than a temperamental inability to yield to the pressure of that epoch even when he perhaps might have wished to do so."[10] Except for one half-hearted attempt to write "correct" poetry in the "required" manner—as in his unsuccesful "Ode to Stalin," not to be confused with his earlier poem ridiculing the Soviet dictator—Mandelstam simply could not raise an authentic poetic voice in harmony with the spirit of the revolutionary era when it became clear to him that the Soviet literary hierarchy abandoned artistic expression in favor of an optimistic and strictly controlled artistic propaganda. Not for his Western-classical bent was the new socialist art preaching the virtue of collective ownership, the efficiency of modern tractors, and the vision of an exemplary country with the new Soviet people working cheerfully together and fulfilling the promises of the future.

Mandelstam's work was virtually unknown in the West until the 1960s when scholars and intellectuals traveling to the Soviet Union began smuggling out of that country some of his writings. Since then books, articles, essays, and critical studies have been appearing with increasing frequency as part of a momentous rediscovery and revaluation, winning for this poet a veritable cult and a reputation of towering proportions. Mandelstam is anything but an easy poet. What makes his poetry recognizable from many other poetic works of the period is not only its great appeal to the collective unconscious of what is most noble and sensitive in the human heart but also the radiant intelligence that triggers this miracle. His creative use of the language, his deliberate ambiguities, his feeling for nuances and ironies that lurk beneath the surface of everyday life, the richness of his emotional associations, his multilevel perceptions, his juxtaposition of the modern world with a mythical age make him tantalizingly difficult. In the modern pantheon of Soviet literature Mandelstam remains the most elusive and problematical of all the poets. As Isaiah Berlin remarked: "The cascades of Mandelstam's glittering or tranquil

22

images leaping out of one another; the historical, psychological, syntactical, verbal allusions, contrasts, collisions, whirling at lightning speed, dazzle the imagination of the intellect."[11] Words may often obtain fresh and unexpected nuances, leading to the possibility of multiple interpretation. Clarence Brown, the distinguished researcher of Mandelstam's life and art, pointed out: "For many of his lines there might be equally correct alternatives. In several poems we are still dealing with approximations."[12] Still another scholar spoke about the emotional and intellectual content of Mandelstam's verse and the great number of concealed quotations from Russian and world literature half-hidden in "his thickets of imagery."[13] The poet is not unlike Degas, who once said that "a painting should keep a certain mystery."

In view of this formidable poetic minefield it appears that an attempt to translate Mandelstam would be like an ascent on the majestic but treacherous slopes of a literary Mont Blanc. Lehmann-Haupt speaks of the impossibility of rendering Mandelstam's poems into English. "We are left with shadows."[14] And, indeed, the great many difficulties of Mandelstam's poetry proved a disaster for many translators, and those pioneering efforts have not served him well in English. The first translators tried hard to meet the challenge by rendering his poetry "straight" and "readable," making it not sound like transplants, and in this cautious pedestrian effort the very soul of the poems was lost. However, between an obstinate loyalty to the literal text of the original at the cost of some occasional pain to contemporary English, as exemplified by Nabokov's "ruthless" account of Pushkin's *Onegin*, and a freewheeling translation—dubbed by some indignant purists as *traduttore traditore*—as, for example, in Robert Lowell's cavalier treatment of some of Mandelstam's poems, there still lies a wide literary pasture to accommodate those who, while respectful of the original without trying to imitate its rhyme and meter, strive to render an honest poetic version in the receiving language.

Fortunately in the last fifteen years this situation has radically improved and continues to improve. Aside from the important *Collected Works (Sobranie sochinenii)*, edited by Gleb Struve and Boris Filippov, 3 volumes (1955–69), the first attempt to bring Mandelstam to the West, the list includes Clarence Brown's *The Prose of Osip Mandelstam* (1965), the same author's *Mandelstam* (1973), Nils Ake Nilsson's essay "Osip Mandelstam and his Poetry," in Edward J. Brown's *Major Soviet Writers* (1973), Clarence Brown and W. S. Merwin's *Selected Poems* (1974), David McDuff's *Selected Poems* (1975), Steven Broyde's *Osip Mandelstam and His Age* (1975), Jennifer Baynes's *Mandelstam The Later Poetry* (1976), Bernard

Meares's *Osip Mandelstam 50 Poems* with an introductory essay by Joseph Brodsky (1977), Ronald Hingley's *Nightingale Fever* (1981), and several scattered translations by Paul Celan and Robert Lowell. These are also the works—together with Boris Pasternak's *Doctor Zhivago* (1958), Albert Camus's *Resistance, Rebellion and Death* (1974), and finally, *Mandelstam, The Complete Critical Prose and Letters,* edited by Jane Gary Harris (1979)—consulted for this introduction.

Still there is no last word on Mandelstam, and, indeed, such a thing as a final statement on poetry simply cannot exist in translation. "A work of art is never finished, but, to paraphrase Paul Valéry, only abandoned."[15] Often the measure of a work's greatness resides in the frequency it is translated. Flaubert's *Madame Bovary* (1857), for example, had been rendered five times into English before Francis Steegmuller wrote his own version, considered the finest, in 1950. There is still much that we do not know and perhaps may never know about Mandelstam. This haunting incompleteness about his chiaroscuro work and its baroque edifice should prompt a desire for further attempts newly to translate and elucidate what this great Russian writer really meant. It would be a literary sin to accept such an artistic casualty without trying to narrow the gap between knowledge and ignorance.

Therefore, a new volume of translations that brings the promise of a fresh point of view, novel insights and perspectives, is certainly welcome news to lovers of poetry and students of literature alike. R. H. Morrison, the translator of the present volume, is a fine, competent, and sensitive artist, whose credentials include a number of impressive publications on Russian, Ukrainian, Italian, Spanish, and even Chinese poetry. He has a sure grasp of the awesome complexities of Mandelstam's poems and, with the elegant touch of a poet, gracefully rendered the ninety-one poems of this collection, faithful and intact, into lucid, contemporary English. This is an unusually valuable addition to the constantly growing number of translations, especially since he offers the reader several poems that, to my knowledge, have never been translated before.

4

Mandelstam began as an heir of Symbolism, but his early literary period coincided with the end of this poetic school and the gradual emergence of Acmeism. The latter was in revolt against the mysticism, impalpability, and remoteness of Symbolism (Mallarmé: "rien que la suggestion") and aimed at returning to the tangible and actual things of this world, as their slogan, "Down with Symbolism. Long live the living rose!" indicated. The Acmeists regarded Shakespeare, Villon, Rabelais, and Théophile Gautier as their mentors. Villon was, for Mandelstam, the most appealing of the four, and he devoted a perceptive essay to the French poet early in his career.

Yet, as some of the poems in *Stone* reveal, he could not immediately cut his umbilical cord to the Symbolists, and his early verses reflect the influence of both. While in one poem such natural objects as "trees," "forests," and "bushes" show the concreteness of Acmeism, the "tinsel gold" and "the toy wolves" with their "fearsome eyes" in the same poem are suggestive of Symbolism (2). Although the poet had seemed to reach a boundary between the two poetic modes of thinking and had already refused to accept the symbol of the moon and all it suggested when the object was in reality only a plain German clock face *(Zifferblatt)* and had found "the loftiness of Batyushkov / repugnant" when he answered "Eternity" to the simple question of "What's the time?" (31), he himself used "eternity" quite often (8, 13, 32.). Thus, while his progression to Acmeism is evident, he continued to oscillate between these two modes for a long time. He was too much aware of "mysterious" life (20) and its "secret way" (19) not to be influenced by Symbolism even in his later poetry. One could say with certainty only that Mandelstam evolved his own special brand of Acmeism over a long period. In an essay "On the Nature of Word" in 1922 he defined Acmeism as "not only a literary but also a social manifestation in Russian history. Together with it a moral force was revived in Russian poetry."[16] And, according to Akhmatova, he said in 1931 that Acmeism was "homesickness for world culture."[17]

One of the creative principles of Mandelstam's art is the clash of two opposites—life versus death, beauty versus horror, and others—which implies a duality, perhaps even a multiplicity, in the poet's viewpoint. Thus, for example, in one poem he knows that he is "fated to die" but also that his "eternity" is decided (499). Here the brevity of human existence contrasts with the eternity of time and being in general. In another (146), death reminds him that he is "living." Life becomes more precious because death is always lurking around ready to strike. Fear of death is created by the anxiety to live. Camus and Sartre would have agreed with this existentialist credo. "There is no love of life without despair of life," said Camus.[18]

The title *Stone*—a proper Acmeist emblem—is a hard, timeless, and everyday object, raw material to build cities, streets, columns, cathedrals, and so on. Many of the poems in this collection contain words stressing the idea of something concrete, as, for example, "swing" (4), "road" (20), "gravestone" (23), "door" (23), "house" (26), "bell-towers" (32), "taverns" (47), "staircase" (55), and such. But these poems also include a radically different vocabulary expressing the concept of something light, tender, and airy, as, for example, "children's books" (4), "light" design (6), "slender" (6), "frail" (7), "silk" (10), "foam" (14), "reed" (17), and such. Even the very title is contradicted in one of his later poems where the poet admits that he "sing[s] not of stone / but of wood . . . about wooden Paradise / where things are so light" (73).

Therefore, as a scholar points out, "This world is not, as the title of the collection would seem to indicate, a solid world where all objects stand firmly in place. It is rather a dualistic world, in which a fatal and uncertain balance reigns."[19] This creates an enduring ambiguity, an existential paradox of a "twofold existence" (22) in which, as in an enigma, all is possible but nothing is certain. It is a Kafkaesque universe: both real and illusory, and the dividing line between the two is blurred.

Yet it is characteristic of the possibility of multiple meaning inherent in Mandelstam's art that this obvious controlling meta-phor—duality—may not be the only explanation. In a poem that begins with the line "I hate the light" (1912), he wishes to reduce "the stone" to "lace" so that it ultimately becomes "a cobweb." This is a transformation and dematerialization of objects, in which the original Acmeist solidity is repeatedly invaded, growing trans-parent, and is finally metamorphosed into something totally and strangely unrelated to the object—stone—with which this puz-zling poetic journey began.

There may be different responses—negative and positive—to the solution of the same problems that agitated Mandelstam throughout his life. Such a problem was the survival of Russian culture, to which the poet devoted a number of poems. Yet he remained ambivalent, and his faith and belief fluctuated between solutions to the problem. In one poem he writes that the victory of art is "short-lived" against "mournful death" (6), but in another, composed shortly thereafter, it is enduring since "the gracious pattern cannot be struck out" (8). The poet's viewpoint might have altered as the changing political environment demanded a fresh approach, a revaluation of his previous position. Still, art's tri-umph remained dominant (354).

Throughout the poems there is a constant sentiment of unease in this "earthly cage" (23) and in this "tedious neighborhood" (67)—obvious allusions to the contemporary world—where there is "so little music / and such tranquillity" (24). It is felt that in the universe's "misty suffering" (22) hope and tolerance became strangers. The world is seen as the "prison" (8) where "strangeness and pain" dominate and the poet is constrained to "take upon" himself its "emptiness" (15). This poem is very close to Pasternak's "Hamlet" and, together with several other poems of Mandelstam, reveals the common strains of an unspoken artistic and human alliance that passed between the two poets. In this atmosphere Mandelstam reaches out toward universal modes of being and perception, toward timelessness and "fundamental life" (14). He seems to be a "traveler" (457, iv) in time, walking an emotional tightrope, an immigrant from a separate planet living in an age different from the eternal age of his muse. With a remarkable poetic sensitivity and inspiration he asks, in a poem in 1914, how soon his "truth" will become "the truth of the people" (69). What often matters in his poems is not the literal sense but the implied potential. It is his imagination, at times difficult for the reader to fathom, that supplies wholeness to the poems.

Sadness, melancholy, silence, and gloom govern the emotional climate of Mandelstam's poems. The word *pechal'* (sorrow, sadness) occurs several times in his early poetry to reflect bareness, emptiness, absence, and depression in his poetic universe. He invokes his "sorrow . . . prophetic sorrow" even in a fairy tale setting (2); "sadness" becomes personalized as it "opened two enormous eyes" (9). The "dark savage soul" can be "both sad . . . and beautiful" (11). In "The Pedestrian" "sadness sings authentically" in the poet (32), and "the sadness" of his people "at home is foreign" to him (69).

Also frequently used is *tuman* (mist) to imply vagueness, distortion, lack of clarity, and uncertainty. He remembers in "misty delirium"—as if in a haze—"the tall, dark spruces" (4). The world's "misty suffering" is reflected by the "wan sky," and the poet himself also wants to be "misty," perhaps to become invisible and escape from this unfriendly world. He cannot "feel" God because of the "mist," a "wreathing vapor of dense mist," (30) in a search for identity and certainty.

Silence—*tishina*—is not only another key word in Mandelstam's vocabulary but also an important motif in his early writings. The word and its derivatives appear as "stillness" (2), "quiet sound" (5), "quiet joy" (8), twilight "quietly" arguing with a ray (24), and "tranquillity" (24). In 15 "unloud" sounds strange in English, but so does *nezvuchnij* in Russian, which previous translators rendered as "unheard," "silent," "hollow" and the like. Morrison did not try to "correct" Mandelstam, but carried over the poet's odd phrase undiluted into English. In most of the poems the word *tishina* has a peaceful, nostalgic ring except in "the tales of Ossian" and

"Scotland's murderous moon," where it is coupled with a negative adjective "sinister silence" (67). In addition to Ossian, Mandelstam might also have had *Macbeth* in mind with the witches ("the roll call of the raven") and Lennox's premonition of the dark events of the king's murder: "The night has been unruly. Where we lay, / Our chimneys were blown down, and, as they say, / Lamentings heard i' th' air, strange screams of death, / And prophesying with accents terrible / Of dire combustion and confused events."[20]

His important poem "Silentium" (14), written in 1910, deserves a deeper look for the light it may throw on the poet's frequent use of this word. One interpretation is that this prophetic bard, with his ears finely attuned to the whisper of the time, already seemed to hear the distant roar of the cannons, the cacophony of the coming war, and was suggesting his preference for peace, quiet, and silence. Poets are often Cassandras of their age. On viewing the strange futuristic images of Picasso, Kafka said that the artist frequently acts like a clock that goes too fast: today he already feels and sees the shapes of things to come tomorrow.

Another explanation is that when, in his poetic search for an overpowering metaphor to express the all, the everything, the grand essence of the cosmos, Mandelstam realized the futility of such a quest, obeying his dualistic nature, he turned to its exact opposite, which he perceived as silence. Silence, the unexpressed, the virgin thought, the raw material of everything, can be utilized as a possible endless source, or an infinite poetic conveyor belt having the potential to express anything. And what is perhaps still more important: that which is not expressed, which stays forever unborn, which remains an unspoken promise, will always survive, since an unexpressed idea cannot wilt, age, or die.

"Heard melodies are sweet, but those unheard / are sweeter" from the "Ode on a Grecian Urn" of Keats—to whom Anna Akhmatova once compared Mandelstam—might have been the source for the poet's predilection for silence, but there is no evidence that he read Keats.

The definite source is the metaphysical Russian poet Fyodor Tyutchev (1803–73), whose influence on Mandelstam is well known. It was Tyutchev's spiritual privacy and the strength of his inner life that inspired Mandelstam to say that Tyutchev was "an expert on life" (undated fragment) and quote him on several occasions. Tyutchev wrote a poem "Twilight" *(Sumerki)* whose title Mandelstam borrowed for his own poem "The Twilight of Freedom."

But most importantly, it is Tyutchev's famous poem "Silentium!" (1833)—this title Mandelstam also borrowed—that inspired Mandelstam to write in the "Nature of Word" that "the old theme of doubting the capacity of the word to express feelings is reiterated in Russian poetry more than in any other poetry."[21] In that poem Tyutchev warned his readers that "an uttered thought is but a lie." Mandelstam might also have been influenced by Nietzsche's *Beyond Good and Evil,* in which the German philosopher says: "Grasp in what has been written a symptom of what has been left unsaid."

The unspoken draws its force and its mystery from its own silence. Less becomes more. A nineteenth century Hasidic teacher put it his own way: the cry unuttered is the loudest. But for the best example we should go to Chinese painting to examine how painting adopts the status and method of poetry . . . "The highest type of pictorial style is called *xie yi,* which means the style that *writes* the *meaning* of things (instead of describing their appearances or shapes). The guiding principle for this form of painting is 'to express the idea without the brush having to run its full course' *(yi da bi bu dao).* The ideal painting is achieved not on paper, but in the mind of the spectator; for the painter, the whole skill consists in selecting those minimal visual clues that will allow the painting to reach its full and invisible blossoming in the viewer's imagination. This point leads us into another theme: the active function of emptiness—the role played by 'blanks' in painting, by silence in music, the poems that lie beyond words."[22]

However, Mandelstam goes beyond his source when he says that "She has not yet been born /. . . . and therefore [she is] the inviolable / bond of everything living." He builds a bridge between the nonexistent and the living cosmos. He prefers a "primordial muteness" to everything in the world because silence is "like a crystalline note / that is pure from birth!" Thus, he even prefers "foam"—which still has the capacity of both becoming anything and surviving in the world—to the beautiful Aphrodite who, after her birth, is already a prisoner of biological laws, unable to change her destiny and doomed to the inevitable process of gradual decay. Therefore, he asks her: "Remain foam, Aphrodite." He also wants the word to lose its wordiness, become mute, and return to music, which is the pristine state of "fundamental life."

Mandelstam's early poetry often has a fairy-tale, dreamy, and hallucinating quality as illusion confronts reality. In one poem trees in the forest are Christmas trees, and the wolves turn out to be toys (2). Even "destiny" seems unreal and "toylike" in another poem (7). There is no symmetry between the two; sometimes illusion and at other times reality dominates. In one poem the illusion created by such phrases as "sadness . . . opened two enormous eyes," "the flower vase awoke," "the whiteness of slenderest fingers / breaking a thin biscuit," and "the whole room was intoxicated" is only imperfectly balanced by the realism of "a little red wine / a little sunshiny May" (9).

One of the main topics of Mandelstam's verses is the solitude of the artist. He travels alone; "sadness sings" in him; there is an "avalanche" in the "mountains" and he is afraid that "music" will not save him (32). The autobiographical details are unmistakable. He is a haunted figure who looks for solace but cannot find it. Yet the poem may also have a symbolic rather than literal meaning. He may be a wanderer through the world of ideas and art, striving to create, like a camera with an inward eye, his own poetic universe. He is "cheerful" in another poem (457, iv) but "no one" leads him "through the valleys" and makes him happy "with the nightingale's murmur." He stays alone "wrapped" in a cloak that "does not warm" yet is "dear" to him—it may be his only property—and takes a poetic "flight along a humble ray / to the commanding stars." The cloak may be a metaphor for solitude: useless yet precious. The unexpressed thought is that Mandelstam deplores the poet's plight in the Soviet Union. The poet's authenticity, so essential to him, is not appreciated so that, faced with indifference and hostility, he must find exile in the mountains to create freely even though life may be dangerous there. Rather a perilous freedom with no one to love and to sing to than an artistic strait jacket.

A similar theme is found in Camus's "The Artist at Work" where Jonas, the gifted painter, finds himself forced to flee society's increasing encroachment to maintain his artistic integrity. A friend visiting him sees a word written on his canvas but cannot decide whether it "should be read *solitary* or *solidary*."[23] The artist's dilemma: stay or run away. Camus feels that he must be, first of all, an artist; a public role may cheapen his artistic integrity and reduce the time he would otherwise devote to his art. Jonas is the biblical man of God whom the whale (society) threatens to swallow.

There are two poems (20, 41) with half-hidden Dostoevskian undertones. An unreal atmosphere dominates the first. The "little light" in the "street lamps" and the mysterious "outlines of dark spruces" create a chiaroscuro effect. Some "strange people" with horses are taking the speaker somewhere. The suspense between two opposing sentiments—his trusting them and his feeling cold (cold is a warning of some disaster), the swaying of his "burning head" and the "tender ice of someone else's hand"—remains unresolved. The poem strongly resembles the end of Dostoevsky's *The Double* where "horses were taking [the hero] along a road he did not know. Dark forest loomed. . . . It was lonely and desolate." He was trembling but showed that he was meek and obedient. His

"fiery blood was rushing to his head."[24] The same hero—Mr. Golyadkin—also appears in Mandelstam's essay "The Egyptian Stamp."[25]

The "green light" in the eyes of the grotesque "Old Man" in the second poem is "either cunning or childlike." He blasphemes, mutters / incoherent words; / he wishes to make confession, / but first of all to sin." He is a "spendthrift" who "plods along" meeting "hilarious trouble" and at home his "stern wife" heaps "abuse" on this "drunken Socrates."

Mandelstam is describing Marmeladov, one of Dostoevsky's grotesque buffoons in *Crime and Punishment* who steals money from his wife, spends it on drinks, and confesses his crime to Raskolnikov in a Petersburg tavern. He is ironically called Socrates because in the novel he holds education "in the highest respect," refers to his wife's scholastic achievements several times, addresses Raskolnikov as a "man of . . . education" who "moved in academic circles," and people in the tavern mock him as "the great intellect." His complexion was "even greenish," and his eyes "had an almost rapturous shine" but also an "assumption of slyness." There is an allusion to a "cunning" trick with which he stole the money. He has a "peculiarly florid manner of speech" that Mandelstam changed—again his love of opposites—to "incoherent words." People snigger and laugh at him—creating a "hilarious trouble"— but also curse and blaspheme. At home Marmeladov's enraged wife "meets him" in a frenzy and abuses him by "clutching his hair [and] dragging him . . . on the floor."[26]

Technically polished, with all the allusory power of sounds, Mandelstam's poetry displays—often in fleeting and fragmentary perceptions—a wide variety of aspects of human culture from Homer (62) and Greek mythology (14) to the Forum and Colonnade of Rome (65) and the misty melancholic tales of Ossian (67), among others.

While art, music, architecture, and cities are significant to the poet as indicating the evolution of his poetic range, it is finally Man himself, the vital creative force in the world, who survives in his art. "The flourishing cities" have only a "fleeting importance," but what is really significant is "man's place in the universe" (66).

5

After 1916—the middle period of his creative activities—Mandelstam's poetic universe underwent several changes, especially in denseness and imagery. Both his thematic and emotional sweep became wider. The contemplative tendency of his early work moved perceptibly toward a faster, more energetic, and more assertive poetic mood. The occasional playful quality and quaint fairy-tale lightness disappeared. There were no more magic wolves; the fragile children's toys were transformed into the real thing. The former abstractions gave way to a nagging foreboding as his response, more mature and innovative than before, to the harsh reality of wars, upheavals, and Russia's new historical path. His two new key words, *vremja* (time) and *vek* (century, age) stressed his involvement and agony but also his sensitivity to future development in his native land. He continued to metamorphose seeing into being. Some of his poems were about single encounters, snapshots of the soul seen with a stranger's curious gaze. Like the *Duino Elegies* of Rilke—to whom he is often compared—his poems seemed written from a great depth within himself: he was speaking out of his own isolation, and his poetry, gaining at times a kind of spiritual plenitude, became religion.

In this period three main themes emerge: the Russian Revolution, the so-called Petersburg tale, and Russian Hellenism.

The attitude of Russian intellectuals to the tumult, promise and terror of the revolution was divided. Some welcomed it, believing that the untapped energy and commitment of the hitherto passive masses might contribute to the enrichment of human life on earth; others left the country in protest, mistrusting the slogans of the Bolsheviks about the beautiful dream of a future human paradise; and still others, the politically unaffiliated heirs of the great nineteenth-century literary tradition—called "fellow travelers" by Trotsky—decided to remain to face a new and alien world.

Scholars disagree on Mandelstam's reaction to this cosmic event. According to Brown, "Mandelstam had welcomed the Revolution . . . but also mistrusted it."[27] Broyde feels that the poet initially held "a violent antipathy" toward the Revolution that "changed over a period of months."[28] An eyewitness of the Revolution, Ehrenburg, writes that, while "poets greeted the Russian Revolution with wild shouts, hysterical tears, laments, enthusiastic frenzy, curses," Mandelstam "alone understood the pathos of the events, comprehended the scale of what was occurring."[29] Brodsky agrees. Mandelstam's was "perhaps the only sober response to the events which shook the world. . . . His sense of measure and his irony were enough to acknowledge the epic quality of the whole undertaking."[30] Yet, most recently, Hingley indicates that the poet was hostile to the upheaval and in a lyric published in a newspaper on 15 November 1917 nicknamed Lenin "October's Upstart" who prepared a "yoke of violence." He even called the armed workers a "vicious rabble."[31]

Mandelstam's most important early reaction to the Russian Revolution was his poem "Twilight of Freedom" (*Sumerki svobody*) published on 24 May 1918 (103). But the poem is ambiguous and the poet is ambivalent. The very title—twilight—may refer to either sunrise or sunset, symbolically to the beginning or the end of an era. The reign of the old regime is called "unhearing years"—other translators have it as "gloomy," "deaf," "dead," "remote," "forlorn," and the like—into which the sun (always a positive, life-giving image in Russian literature and often a symbol for Pushkin in Mandelstam's poetry), the judge, and the people "are rising." This is a clash of opposites: the rising sun of the revolution overwhelms the old Tsarist rule.

The juxtaposition of judges and people may show Pushkin's influence. In his historical drama *Boris Godunov*, the people's voice—*vox populi*—is the final arbiter in deciding the outcome of the civil war between the adherents of Boris and the partisans of the alleged Dimitry (Scene 21, Headquarters.) The reference to the "tears" and "the somber burden of power, / its insupportable weighing-down" with which the new leader assumes his responsibilities may also be a Pushkinian echo from the same drama when Boris, ascending the throne, "accept[s] the greatest power," exclaiming, "How heavy is the obligation on me!" in order to indicate the emotional and spiritual weight of the new tsar's duties (Scene 4, the Kremlin Palace.[32]) The "nation's leader" is undoubtedly Lenin, a radical change from the poet's calling him, just seven months ago in an antagonistic poem, "October's Upstart."

Yet is Lenin praised here? The parallel between him and Boris Godunov is fraught with highly ominous implications. In Pushkin's drama Boris is accused of having reached the Russian throne by instigating the murder of Tsarevich Dimitry, the youngest son of Ivan the Terrible and the legitimate heir to the crown; and Mandelstam alludes to this gruesome event in a poem beginning with the words "On the sledge . . ." written in March 1916. Even today, almost four hundred years after his death in 1605, Boris has remained the most controversial figure in Russian history. Although several historians in this century—Platonov and Vernadsky among others—absolved him of ordering the Tsarevich's murder, with one exception—*The Loyal Subject*, a play by John Fletcher, Shakespeare's contemporary, staged in 1618—there is no drama, novel, or poem in the huge orchard of Russian and world literature on the theme in which he would not appear as the villain. He is often called the Russian Machiavelli, Cromwell, or even Richard III, all advocates of violence to grab power.

Thus, if the Pushkinian reference is accepted as a source, the comparison may suggest that Lenin had gained power through fraudulent means and therefore the humane origin and idealism of the Russian Revolution is compromised. A morally impure Lenin/Boris could only lead the nation to troubles and disturbances. This hypothesis may reflect the intellectual turmoil of the poet suffering from his own crisis of faith. The poet's view finds support in recent years among the Soviet intelligentsia who feel that "Leninism was fatally flawed from the start by totalitarianism."[33]

But in the second stanza we also read that the "ship" of "time" is sinking. Time—historical time—must be seen as a symbol for the old regime whose "time" is up and its "ship"—in the sense of its reign—is now going under as a result of the victorious revolution. If we can afford to ignore the Lenin/Boris parallel, the two important symbols of the poem so far—the rising sun of the revolution and the sinking ship of the old regime—would produce a positive effect in favor of the new world in Russia. Which explanation can we believe?

What did the poet mean in the third stanza: "We have bound the swallows together / in battle legions, and behold, / no sun is seen"? In Russian literature swallows often stand for people, and when they are bound—united—in "battle legions" they represent a strong—here revolutionary—army. But how can a revolutionary army darken—threaten—the rising sun, the very symbol of the revolution? This would not make sense. And why did the poet repeat the phrase "no sun is seen" as if to underline the constancy and continuity of the threat? We have to stretch our imagination to hazard a guess in two opposite directions. In the medieval epic "The Lay of Igor's Raid" (*Slovo o polku Igoreve*), whose "lively and image-laden" artistry the poet praised,[34] the sun plays an important role. In preparing his campaign Prince Igor sees "the bright sun" and then his warriors "enveloped in darkness" and, later in the prairie, finds that "the sun barred his way with darkness." (We know that there was an eclipse of the sun on 1 May 1195, at the time of Igor's campaign.) This was regarded as an "evil omen" and Igor lost. Thinking of this poem and its relevance to the present, the poet reversed the "evil omen"—we recall his preference for dualities—and had the mass of armed workers make the sun invisible by their presence, a poetic hyperbole, stressing, as he did in another poem (88), "man's" important "place in the universe" and implying his vital part in the creation of the new world. In the purity of its conception the Russian Revolution was considered a hymn to man.

A radically opposite guess is that the swallows, darkening the sun of the revolution, represent the Whites. In the civil war the white armies, assisted by foreigners, fought the Bolsheviks for three and a half years and seriously threatened the establishment and consolidation of their power in Russia.

It is only at the end of the poem—in the fourth stanza—that the poet tilts in a clear, positive direction—this time without the possibility of a different interpretation—as he decides to give a chance to the new regime, still young and groping in the dark, to establish itself: "Let us make the attempt." Even though the rudder is "lumbering and creaking," he calls on the people to accomplish the job: "Courage, men!" Mandelstam implies that simple human beings are superior to the tsars and the great nobles whom they replace. He also reminds them never to forget what a heavy price they paid for this effort: "the cost of the earth . . . was ten heavens." Yet the earth—the *hic* and *nunc*—is more important than the nebulous heaven of tomorrow just as previously man was more important than the sun. The Kingdom of Man is the earth for Mandelstam, and now man and his earth equal the revolution. Yet while the word "revolution" has a noble, almost sacred ring, where should we look in retrospect: at the inspiration or the results? Mandelstam might have felt that, although the word "revolution" is still revered, belief that it can deliver the promised land on earth has ebbed.

It is this positive ending that ties Mandelstam's poem to Blok's masterpiece "The Twelve," often called the hymn of the revolution, where twelve red guards quarrel, plunder, and kill as they march through the snow and frost until, at the end, Christ suddenly appears at their head as if to restore peace and order, bless them, and lead them to victory. Mandelstam found Blok's poem "immortal as folklore is immortal."

Is "Twilight of Freedom" a kind of a Wagnerian *Goetterdaemmerung,* an apparently everlasting enigma reminiscent of the composer's *Ring of the Niebelung* cycle, a conflict between love and lust for power that can be explained in so many contradictory ways? It is interesting to note that, aside from their different epochs, the historical and political geneses of the Wagnerian opera and of Mandelstam's poem display distinct similarities. Wagner first began working on the cycle in 1848, the year of the *Communist Manifesto,* when revolutions were spreading like prairie fires across Euorpe, monarchs cowered, and chancelleries trembled, raising hopes of democracy and an end to special privilege. The vision of a better world hung precariously in the balance at this midpoint between the French and the Russian Revolution. Yet the three great Wagnerian interpreters—Nietzsche, Shaw, and Thomas Mann—all read the *Ring of the Niebelung* differently. The culprit was Wagner himself who deliberately mystified the opera lovers by writing the librettos of the four parts in reverse order while composing the music in narrative sequence. Defending his method, he wrote in a letter: "I believe it was a sound instinct which set me on my guard against . . . making everything clear, for I have come to the firm conclusion that to make my intention too obvious would get in the way of a genuine understanding.[35] Donal Henahan calls this "an appeal to the uncertainty principle."[36]

As a philosophical poem Mandelstam's "Twilight of Freedom" deals with the limit of logic and the possibilities of artifice. It may encapsulate a truth within an illusion. It may be an illustration of how difficult liberty is to grasp and how easily it slips away. Yet it is—consciously or subconsciously—so thoroughly saturated with ambiguities that a final statement—a tidy explication—may just not be possible. Does the positive fourth stanza redeem the doubts, uncertainties, and possibly sinister implications of the other three? Is Russia now free to evolve in a constructive direction? Now that the tsar is thrown out, has the earth been sufficiently cleansed and purified so that a reign of fraternity may confidently begin? What do we glorify here, the sun or the darkness, freedom or chaos, revolution or counterrevolution, reality or illusion? Is it a triumphant hymn or a funeral dirge? Does Mandelstam still continue his never-ending poetic peregrination between Acmeism (the real sun that shines, warms, and eclipses) and Symbolism (the sun as hope, promise, and strength of the revolution) as he is trying to capture the essence of those *Ten Days That Shook The World* (John Reed's account of the Russian Revolution)? Does art have a greater truth than life? Does it expose what history often conceals, forgets, or mutilates? Does the power of the poet's images depend on his ambiguities? Unable to decide whether what we see here is a face or a mask, we return to this puzzling poem again and again to plumb the depth of Mandelstam's substratum. Even the way the title is translated may already suggest a slight bias. Most translators have rendered it as "twilight," but Hingley used "half-light," which might have further deepened the mystery, while Broyde had it as "dawn," which seemed to "err" on the side of a positive interpretation. Perhaps all one can do is to imply some strategies, suggest mental moods, and indicate possibilities. Influenced by this use of artifice and by the way Mandelstam plays the game of reality, we may find ourselves thinking *Right You Are If You Think You Are* as the title of one of Pirandello's plays asserts. If beauty is in the eyes of the beholder, in this poem's marvellous depth and resonance Mandelstam's elusive truth may often become the reluctant—albeit transitory—prisoner of his interpreters. The poem is a classic of political and cultural obscuration.

Finally, it might be useful to point out that much of the interpretation of this poem depends on the time in which it is read. Shakespeare's *Hamlet,* for example, in agreement with the way directors and actors sensed the ideas of their particular epoch, has been played in various manners: a critical melodrama, a drama of metaphysics, a lesson in Viennese psychoanalysis, and so on. Similarly, Chekhov's *The Cherry Orchard* has also been performed both in a serious and in a comic vein, as a forerunner of land reform under the Bolsheviks or as an example of the frivolous way that the former absentee landlords lived, depending on the conception of the actors and directors at a particular moment in history. Thus, as *Hamlet* or *The Cherry Orchard,* "The Twilight of Freedom" can also be regarded as a mirror of the times.

If there were any doubts about Mandelstam's attitude to the Russian Revolution after his poem "Twilight of Freedom," an essay "Humanism and the Present," written five years later in 1923 for Alexey Tolstoy's newspaper *On The Eve* in Berlin, made his position absolutely clear. "There are epochs which contend that they care nothing for man, that he is to be used like brick or cement, that he is to be built with, not for. . . . How is one to guard the human dwelling against the terrible tremors, how to ensure its walls against the subterranean shocks of history? . . . No laws about the rights of man . . . can any longer ensure the human dwelling. . . . The future is cold and terrifying for whoever fails to understand this. . . . If the social architecture of the future does not have as its basis a genuinely humanistic justification, it will crush man."[37]

This essay reflected his growing fear of the dark side of Soviet power. Brown calls it "a moving essay . . . of a doomed intellectual humanism seeking not to adjust its moral values to those of the revolution but rather to assert them one last time."[38] Mandelstam could no longer believe that the Russian Revolution was the locomotive of history and an accomplished model for humanity's progress.

Because of the remarkable artistic affinity between Mandelstam and Pasternak, his great contemporary, it is worth while to compare "Twilight of Freedom" and some of Mandelstam's later poems with Pasternak's *Doctor Zhivago,* the most celebrated Russian novel of the century, in order to see how similar are the reactions of the two writers to the cosmic events of the revolution.

Mandelstam's doubts, vacillations, ambivalences, and final rejection of Stalinism are clearly mirrored in the apocalyptic journey of Yury Zhivago, Pasternak's hero. Having just returned from the front in 1917, he welcomes the February Revolution, calling the events "unprecedented, extraordinary . . . tremendous, titanic . . .

Russia is destined to be the first socialist state since the beginning of the world."[39]

Yet at the same time he "could not rid himself of the sadness that oppressed him," and "did not know where to escape from his forebodings of disaster." Later he looks "upon himself and his milieu as doomed. . . . Ordeals were ahead, perhaps death. . . . He realized that he was a pigmy before the monstrous machine of the future."[40]

However, still later on in 1917, when news of the October Revolution reached Moscow as he walked in a blizzard trying to read a newspaper report of the new events, the novel editorializes: "But it was not the snowstorm that prevented him from reading. The historic greatness of the moment moved him so deeply that it took him some time to collect himself." And shortly afterwards he reflects on the new revolutionary decrees: "What splendid surgery! You take a knife and with one masterful stroke you cut out all the old stinking ulcers. Quite simply, without any nonsense you take the old monster of injustice . . . and sentence it to death. This fearlessness, this way of seeing the thing through to the end, has a familiar national look about it. It has something of Pushkin's uncompromising clarity and of Tolstoy's unwavering faithfulness to the facts . . . This new thing, this marvel of history, this revelation, is exploded right into the very thick of daily life without the slightest consideration for its course. . . . That's real genius. Only real greatness can be so unconcerned with timing and opportunity."[41]

Yet after this enthusiastic praise for the first act of the revolution, almost without any transition, in the very first line of the next chapter he complains about the threatening existential reality of his life: the "dark, hungry, and cold" winters, "the inhuman efforts to cling to life as it slipped out of your grasp, the commissars who come "invested with dictatorial powers . . . armed with means of intimidation and guns . . . [who] knew the slinking bourgeois breed . . . and spoke to them without the slightest pity . . . as to petty thieves caught in the act."[42] The moral and physical condition of his family becomes worse and worse. "They were tried to the limit of their endurance. They had nothing and they were starving."[43] Shortly thereafter Yury contracts typhus, almost dies, and when he recovers, his family decides to leave Moscow for the Urals.

It is during this journey that his final disillusion with the revolution sets in. His father-in-law recalls: "Do you remember the night you brought me the paper with the first government decrees in the winter . . . ? You remember how unbelievably uncompromising they were? It was that single-mindedness that carried us away.

But such things retain their original purity only in the minds of those who have conceived them, and then only on the day they are first made public. Next day the casuistry of politics has turned them inside out. What can I say to you? Their philosophy is alien to me, their regime is hostile to us . . ."[44]

In a conversation with another traveler Yury explains his opinion about Marxism: "Marxism is too uncertain of its grounds to be a science. Sciences are more balanced, more objective. I don't know a movement more self-centered and further removed from the facts than Marxism. Everyone is worried only about proving himself in practical matters, and as for the men in power, they are so anxious to establish the myth of their infallibility that they do their utmost to ignore the truth. . . . I don't like people who don't care about the truth."[45]

In conclusion, it is important to point out that, while Mandelstam's "Twilight of Freedom" was written in 1918, Pasternak began working on *Doctor Zhivago* in 1945. In Hingley's words: "It took him (Pasternak) nearly thirty years to arrive at the definitive conclusion that the society thrown-up by Russia's October Revolution had taken a tragically mistaken road. But Yury Zhivago is described as reaching a comparable pitch of disillusion almost immediately after the Bolshevik take-over of 1917, and this despite the early enthusiasm for revolution which he is portrayed as sharing with his creator."[46] Thus, it is clear that the young Pasternak was far from being disillusioned with the revolution and, judging from the poems he wrote about Stalin and Lenin, his political reactions kept changing until the composition of his novel. As Hingley notes: ". . . he had embarked in the early 1920s on the hesitant and meandering course of one who sporadically flirted with, supported, rejected, and ignored the increasingly insistent demands put forward by authority in the name of the new society. He had hymned Russia's revolutionary past in some poems, and had derided it by implication in others. . . . But never . . . had he come near to achieving stability and consistency in his political thinking."[47] The turning point came in 1945 when he reached a mature political viewpoint and made a decisive break with Stalinism.

Reading *Doctor Zhivago* we are struck by the moving, epic scenes and the authentic sounds of the grand historical panorama in the morning of the revolution. But it is not the voice of the young Pasternak who reports the events. It is the voice of the disillusioned older Pasternak who towards the end of his tortuous spiritual Odyssey "meets" the young Mandelstam in this intellectual and political metamorphosis.

Petersburg—later Petrograd (Mandelstam often called it by the

39

classical name of Petropolis) and today Leningrad—was built by Peter the Great, an emperor with an unlimited ambition, finished in 1724, in a forsaken, weather-tortured, malaria-ridden swamp. Peter saw it as a symbol of his quest to modernize his nation and as an observation post to see and hear all that was going on in Europe. But, as the Russians are fond of saying, this "window to the West" was built on the blood of the peasants as hundreds of his construction workers were drowned in this enterprise. Yet the equestrian statue of this tsar is always covered with flowers left by the common people. In Russian literature the city retained this double aspect: positive because of its cultural and technological contribution to the growth of Russia and negative because of the tremendous sacrifice of human lives in its construction. It is an uncertain legacy. Leningrad, not unlike Paris, is a city whose fabric is a celebration of its own history.

Although other writers also had written of the painful birth of the city before him, the Petersburg theme really begins with Pushkin's "The Bronze Horseman," a philosophical poem on state power and individual rebellion. While paying high tribute in this poem to Peter the Great, the Tsar-carpenter, for building this beautiful city and expanding the glory of Russia, Pushkin is grieved because Yevgeny, a low clerk, loses his bride in the general devastation caused by the flooding of the Neva, accuses the Tsar of negligence, "threatens" his statue, and dies when this statue "pursues" him. In his humanistic sentiment that, despite the erection of this majestic city, the death of a simple man still mattered, Pushkin feels sorrow: "I have a sad tale to tell."

But, more than anything else, it is the city of Dostoevsky, who hated the West and felt that all the corrupting influences of Europe destroying the pure Russian soul came through the Westernized city of Petersburg. He calls it "the most abstract and intentional city" in *Notes From the Underground* and believes that the strange "intellectual" murder committed by his superman Raskolnikov in *Crime and Punishment* could only have happened in this crime-ridden, nihilistic and un-Russian city.

Although not born there, Mandelstam affectionately and proudly regarded Petersburg as his native city. "I returned to my city—familiar to tears," he said when, after a long absence, he went back to Petersburg in 1930. He considered the city the spiritual and cultural center of the Russian Empire and the cradle of Russian poetry and prose. This classical eighteenth-century city, devised by Italian architects, with its memorable buildings, canals, and long straight streets disappearing into northern infinity inspired the poet with a "kind of childish imperialism" and a sense of national consciousness.[48]

40

Mandelstam's artistic response to the dramatic history of the city can be found in his youthful prose memoir "The Noise of Time" (1910), in which he contrasts the mediocrity and provincialism—indeed, his inner experience of the death of Russian culture—of the present with the glory and greatness of the past. This essay is so specifically personal in its powerful emotional and literary range as to present a fascinating look into that peculiar psychological bond which existed between the young intellectual and his "beloved" Petersburg. The world is seen with the innocent eyes of a nineteen-year-old youth, growing up in the midst of the architectural splendor of this elegant city, which was "completely out of keeping with the kitchen fumes of a middle class apartment . . . [and] Jewish conversation about business."[49]

He paints a multicolored panorama of the "sacred and festive" Kazan Cathedral "with its forest of bullet-ridden banners" captured from Napoleon; the Admiralty building, where beauty is the dream not of some demi-god but of a carpenter's cunning eye; numerous churches, squares, and "shaggy" parks; the May parade where he "envied the very boards themselves"; the Summer Garden with its "Babylonian uproar of hundreds of orchestras"; and also such modest sights of Dutch Petersburg as grocery stores, bakeries, watchmakers, and pharmacists.[50]

A multitude of literary references are scattered around, yet inwardly bound together, and memorable heroes of fiction come suddenly alive as they weave in and out of his nostalgic and whimsical prose. "Every time Russians speak, their ancestors speak too. It is a profound feeling in the heart and in the stomach."[51] He reacquaints us with Pushkin's *Covetous Knight* and *Ruslan and Lyudmila*, makes us walk again on Gogol's luminous *Nevsky Prospect*, and reopens the pages of *Dead Souls*. The atmosphere of the railroad station and the music concert at Pavlovsk, a suburb of Petersburg—almost forgotten yet so familiar from Dostoevsky's *The Idiot*—is back with us. We reexperience the love and honor that Nikolenka Rostov seeks on the battlefield as *War and Peace* "goes on," and Prince Andrey continues "to gaze into the blank sky" with his cold, astonished eye, except that, as the young Mandelstam sadly remarks, "the glory had moved elsewhere."[52] This remarkable evocation of a wide gallery of Russian literary figures also includes Lermontov's Pechorin (*A Hero of Our Times*), Turgenev's Bazarov (*Fathers and Sons*), and such motifs as Fet's nightingales and Blok's *Puppet Show* among others. Extending his literary range, Mandelstam also makes allusions to such great names in world literature as Shakespeare, Goethe, Schiller, Molière, Balzac, Hugo, Ibsen, and Maeterlinck.

It always seemed to Mandelstam that in this historical city

41

"something very splendid and solemn was absolutely bound to happen," but then he comes back to earth with the painful realization that "all the elegant mirage of Petersburg was merely a dream, a brilliant covering thrown over the abyss" (the word abyss is a loan from Tyutchev who uses it repeatedly) "while round about there sprawled the chaos of Judaism."[53] It is difficult to imagine a greater absurdity than this pathetic one-sided love affair between this dreaming, awkward, and pensive little Jewish boy and the mighty capital of the huge Russian Orthodox Empire. It is Don Giovanni played by Woody Allen reading Freud. One cannot help thinking also of Chaplin in such poignantly bitter-sweet films as *Gold Rush* and *City Lights* where the spectators cry and laugh almost simultaneously, to understand this tender, comic, and pitiful contrast. Not surprisingly, "the figure of Chaplin appealed to him immensely."[54]

In his Petrograd cycle of poems—two of which are included in this volume—a sense of impending doom dominates as the poet feels that this city—a symbol of the whole Russian Empire and its culture—is on the edge of a catastrophe. The death motif is hinted at in one poem (88), in which the words "transparent" and "dragon-flies" are not mere suggestions but by now established literary symbols of death in Mandelstam's poetry. We may interpret the coming of spring, together with his "feeling cold"— remembering that this poem was written in 1916 in the midst of a long, bloody war—as the poet's hope that peace will finally arrive and his apprehension that he may not live to see it. The reference to the river Neva—often called black Neva in his poetry—which disgusts him like a "medusa," may have an antecedent in Pushkin's "The Bronze Horseman," where the river is blamed for the disaster it caused "over darkened Petrograd" with its "boisterous billows" and is even compared to a "bandit" who bursts upon a village "to smash and slay, destroy and pillage." In the poems of both Pushkin and Mandelstam, the Neva is shown as dangerous and destructive. This existential *angst* is even more strongly felt in another poem—beginning with the line "At a fearful height . . . ," written in 1918—with its haunting refrain "Your brother, Petropolis, is dying."

While in this poem (88) there is a suggestion that the poet might not survive, in the next one (89) Mandelstam specifically spells out the terrible destiny of the people: "we'll die" in "the transparent city." Athena, the compassionate goddess of wisdom and arts, whose statue stands in the Admiralty building that the poet so much admired, would presumably have protected him and his friends, but she has been dethroned by the cruel Proserpine (the Latin form of Persephone), the queen of the underworld, the wife of Hades; and therefore "we drink in mortal air / and every hour to us is mortal time." We are here witnessing a battle of mythological goddesses—perhaps a reference to the current war between Russia and Germany—that will destroy Petropolis and its population.

Mandelstam's abiding interest in Petersburg and the personality of Peter the Great is reflected by his half-hidden allusions to this Emperor in several of his poems. In "The Finder of a Horseshoe" (1923) there is a reference to "the father of voyages" and "seafarers' friend," who is obviously Peter the Great, a traveler in Western Europe and builder of the first Russian fleet. In "Ariosto" (1936) the poet speaks of "power" that is "hideous like a barber's hand," an allusion to the Emperor's much publicized custom of personally shaving off the beards of his noblemen to make them look more civilized at his court.

According to Brodsky[55] Russian Hellenism grew out of a sense of cultural inferiority toward the West because of the country's geography, which is neither East nor West, and because of its imperfect history. As a result, Russian men of letters pursued the ideal of a certain cultural unity nursed by an intellectual hunger for the enlightening currents of the West. Due to its advantageous location Petersburg became a clearing house for these currents and was instrumental in developing a blend of Hellenic and native Russian culture. A detailed treatment of Mandelstam's unusually rich references to classical mythology is outside the scope of this introduction. But without some general observations and a few examples at least, something very precious for the understanding of his art would be lost.

From his early years Mandelstam was keenly interested in Greek and Roman antiquity. The fifteen-year-old student already wanted to write a paper "on the reasons for the fall of the Roman Empire."[56] With the passage of time he was more and more devoted to the tradition of Hellenic culture, while retaining, at the same time, his native intellectual roots. Especially strongly did he oppose wars, upheavals, and social injustice in what Nadezhda Mandelstam called an "insane epoch when all the principles of social life, all the foundations of European—and consequently of Russian—culture were being eradicated"[57] by celebrating the order and culture of the classical world.

Much of Mandelstam's creative art was centered around historical allegories, especially classical ones. In every sense he was a nostalgic classicist. In this volume he mentions Aphrodite (14), Socrates (41), Homer (62), the Acropolis (84), Athena (89), Antigone (113), Persephone (116), Euripides (178), the Pleiades (457), and several times Rome (65, 66, 69, 184, among others). These classical references evoke the beauty and power of the Mediterranean tradition and its myths as they, in turn, reaffirm the vitality and spirituality of his own poetry.

During the Russian Revolution the poet spent some time in the Crimea, which, with its sharply delineated coastlines, sun-drenched islands, and gentle blue waves offering a vivid contrast to the foggy, misty, and sunless north, was sacred territory to him because it was once part of the ancient Greek world. In a poem written in 1917 beginning with the line "The stream of golden honey . . ." the poet speaks of Bacchus, god of wine; the white columns; the grapes reminding him of "battles fought long ago / where curly riders struggled"; of the "woman everyone loved"— not Helen, but "the other" (he means Penelope); and he dreams of the expedition of the Argonauts to capture the Golden Fleece that sailed to Colchis where the sea waves sang and "Odysseus returned" to his wife. These wonderful, happy days, reminiscent of the Golden Age of antiquity, make him forget the chaos of the revolution.

The poet saw significant crossfertilization between history and mythology as part of the eternal process of the transformation of the universe. In his poetry the world of nature often changes into the world of myth and vice versa. Mandelstam regarded myths as more than just learned material handed down by tradition. The gods of Greece and the Mediterranean offered him substance and form for his poetic enterprise. Sometimes he even used the rich harvest of classical mythology as artistic camouflage by masking current events and historical figures in the shimmering robe of mythology. Time and again there are references to the ancient Greek world as the poet himself seeks role models to explain the meaning of, and even to find help in, his often hapless personal situation. In a poem beginning with the line "I did not ward off your embraces. . . ," written in 1920, for example, the unhappy love the poet felt for the actress Olga Arbenina is acted out in a mythological setting. In *Odyssey* 4, Menelaus tells of how the cunning Helen, suspecting Greek warriors hidden inside the wooden horse, walked around it three times and, imitating their wives' voices, called out to them. In the poem Mandelstam does not spell out Helen's name, but speaks of a "seductive image" who appears in the warriors' dreams three times. The additional reference to "dear Troy" and "the royal house" that will be demolished hints at the sad conclusion of the poet's romance. In another poem, which begins with "I will tell you frankly . . ."—written in 1930(?)—the poet contrasts the victorious Greek expedition against Troy for "beauty's sake" with his own insecure situation as "shame" looks at him "through dark holes."

Mandelstam found that myths, in their true sense, are the reenactment of a religious experience applicable to the present. They have the power of transforming his everyday reality into a different world where, meeting gods and goddesses, he may make mythological patterns part of his creative experience. Thus, as Stanley Kunitz said, "old myths, old gods, old heroes never died. They are only sleeping at the bottom of our mind, waiting for our call. We have need of them. They represent the wisdom of our age."[58] Therefore, it often seems as if these myths were the symbolic baggage of Mandelstam's subconscious mind and a manifestation of his not yet fully formulated thoughts as they reecho throughout his art to add further nuances and resonances to the content of a previous poem. This way they tend to become his own personal archetypes. While the old gods may not always show up by name, they are there, by their spirit and characteristics, in the key episodes of the poet's life and art.

6

"In the room of the outlawed poet / His fear and muse stand guard by turn / While night approaches / With no hope of dawn." The pattern of interplay between his anxiety and his art in these four lines of a poem Akhmatova wrote when she visited the exiled Mandelstam in 1936 best characterizes the terrible situation of the poet in the last—so-called Voronezh—period. It is an Orwellian nightmare as one accepts tension and fear, the psychological effects of brutal repression, as a normal state of existence. In this poem Akhmatova correctly predicted the horrors of the following years, when Stalin declared war on the Russian intellectual community and "squandered its poets."[59]

"The most terrible thing in the Voronezh poems—and in some pre-Voronezh ones"—writes Wladimir Weidlé, a literary critic, "is that there may be sensed in them a spiritual torment which passes the limits of what can find utterance in art; that torment which shatters art."[60] Henry Gifford adds that "Pasternak was to feel something of that anguish near the end of his life when the storm broke over *Doctor Zhivago*."[61]

The Voronezh period was the harshest phase of Mandelstam's exile; these were the years of visionary intensity in his mature poetic life when all his previous themes gave way to a never-ending foreboding with a pathos not found in any of his earlier works. He was like Lorca, another of his contemporaries, death-haunted. His lyric fatalism, superstition in respect of omens, his obsession with assassination and suicide, had a personal ring. Yet it also revealed how art helped him gain a sense of his power to shape the final moments of his life. This passion for creation, for fresh images and ideas, was also an ecstatic embodiment of his own identity: a personal and creative fusion. This evolution, almost unprecedented in modern literature, lent his writing an intense radiance and spiritual power. Like Isaac Babel, a Soviet short-story writer who shared his fate in one of Stalin's camps, Mandelstam possessed an ability to describe events of shocking brutality with a simplicity and concision that served to heighten rather than diminish their impact on the reader. The dark under-current of Stalinism has been refracted through the sensibility of the poet.

This obsessive fear already began before his exile. In one poem "Leningrad" (December 1930) he returns to the city only to find himself haunted with the idea of death. "I do not want to die yet," he protests. He feels a stranger in his "native" city because all the addresses he has are of friends already dead, and at night he waits for his "dear nocturnal guests" to arrest him. The controlling device of his early poetry—contrast—can still be found in the difference between a fine door chain on his home and a solid heavy chain to be used by his "guests" when they handcuff and take him to prison. In another poem (223) he begs God to "suc-cor" him to survive "this night" because he "fear[s]" for his "life," since living in this city is "like sleeping in a coffin." The brevity of this poem—only three lines—reinforces his abject fear and hope-lessness. The reference to the coffin recalls Raskolnikov living in a coffinlike room. The Petersburg that he liked so much is gone forever, and the city has become a death chamber with its stultify-ing atmosphere. The poem is the short prayer of a man sentenced to die.

It is impossible to do justice in a few lines to the simple beauty, radiance, and despair of these last poems. The few examples that follow show his reflections—as observer, commentator, and vic-tim—on his own situation and the contemporary Soviet reality.

In a poem (336)—written in December 1936—Mandelstam has to confront a rather strange winter in Voronezh. The deceptively casual beginning "winter / is a belated gift" cannot mask the poet's apprehension of "its uncertain sweep," for who can tell what will happen to him? Winter is not only the season of the year, but the time of destitution serving "as an alarm" to warn him of the "stern deeds," the precursor of terror that sends a shudder down his spine. The bleak picture is made more hopeless by a "treeless cycle" when even the "raven's grown timid" and "rivulets" speak "without sleep."

Equally frightening is the beginning of the next poem (341), in which death is universalized. "Mounds of human heads recede into the distance" seems to indicate that so many people have perished already that the pain of discovery is replaced by insensitive statistics. Perhaps he recalled the paintings of Vasily Vereshchagin, a Russian artist at the time of the Russo-Turkish war, showing a mountain of human skulls over which big black birds wheel back and forth. It is no longer headline news. It is as if the poet himself has already accepted his inevitable death as a simple fact of the inflexible human condition. If so many have already died—as in an anonymous slaughter—what does it matter that he, too, is "diminishing" and that soon his absence will not even be "noticed." Yet, as an unexpected light in the dark, the next two lines are full of hope. The poet gains strength and faith from the knowledge that he will not fully die but will continue to live "in warm-hearted books," a fine phrase by Morrison, and "in children's games." This is the spiritual legacy of the poet: an enduring vision of the victory of art over mere earthly existence. This has always been a favorite theme of the poet, and he expressed the same thought in several of his youthful poems (6, 8, 26.) The inspiration might have come from Gautier, admired by the Acmeists as their forerunner, who in "L'Art" (1832) said "Tout passe—L'art robuste / Seul à l'éternité / Le buste / Survit à la cité." The American poet Henry Austin Dobson expressed it even better "All passes. Art alone / Enduring stays to us; / The bust outlasts the throne— / The coin, Tiberius."[62] But Pushkin could also have been the source because he wrote in his poem "Exegi Monumentum" (1836) "No, I shall never die; the sacred lyre / Outlives the dust. / Its echoes shall inspire / The final poet, who in silence hears / My voice unchanged through all the changing years."[63] Or perhaps Horace, whose idea it was, whose words Pushkin cites and whom Mandelstam knew.

Mandelstam often sought identification with the humiliated victims of a crushing reality, and therefore it is only natural that he commiserates with the "beatenness" of the plains whose miserable condition reflects the oppressive climate of the country (350). In this and other poems about nature the landscape, as it often happens in Russian literature, is alive with meaning; it is a place in Mandelstam's poetry where human suffering has been certified as real and thus landscape is not just an unimportant scenic backdrop but a concrete artistic force. Mandelstam often creates a bleak landscape which is haunting and unresolved. But that unresolved landscape represents a powerful statement of a cataclysm to come which will pollute and degrade the environment and leave a naked, empty world behind. Thus, Mandelstam's landscapes may be seen as the symbolic heart of Russia.

But the poet's advocacy of the unspoilt country as noble has also something to do with his distrust of the much-vaunted scientific progress of the Soviet Union—a distrust he inherited from the intellectual tradition of the Roman poets. He might also have been influenced by Ibsen whom he admired as a symbolist. "At the age of fifteen I passed through the purging fire of Ibsen," he wrote to V. V. Gippius in 1908.[64] As an aficionado of the theater he surely saw Ibsen's *The Enemy of the People,* often shown at the Moscow Art Theater, in which Dr. Stockman defends the purity of public water supply against a group of greedy individuals. In this connection it may be worth while to recall the reflections of the French Jesuit thinker Pierre Teilhard de Chardin on our evolutionary progress who argued that we have to make an appropriate moral advance in step with our scientific advances lest our discoveries turn to our destruction. But one thinks of Thoreau first who found in nature's ruin the metaphor of man's self-betrayal. Mandelstam might also have been struck by the similarity between Dr. Stockman's last statement in the drama ". . . the strongest man in the world is he who stands most alone,"[65] and his own lonely position in the hostile Soviet world, and received moral encouragement from it.

Thus, it is easy to understand that the line in this poem (350) "Whither and whence are they?" is really asking a question about Russia's identity and future. Although not mentioned by name, Stalin appears twice in the poem. First as an evil spirit who, with his murderous nature, destroyed the country, and then as "the Judas" who "slowly creep[s]" across Russia and betrays the people of the present and future who "cry out" in their sleep. The wicked emperor remains naked.

It is interesting to look at the next poem (352) because it was written at the time when the poet, driven to total despair, for once in his life, however reluctantly, wrote the "Ode to Stalin" for the sake of sheer physical survival. Thus the mood of this poem is influenced by the atmosphere of the "ode," a kind of forced resignation. The poet previously made some comparisons between his flat steppe and Tuscany, as if planning for a future trip—or was it just a poetic fancy?—to that beautiful land. Yet the trip to the Mediterranean civilization never took place. The poet made peace with his surroundings—in political code he bowed to the reality—and decided just to wander around "the still young Voronezh hills."

48

Although both the next (354) and the previous poem were written in January 1937 there is a distinctly different mood in the latter. "Still I have not yet died" asserts the poet, recovering his pride and accepting his "serene and comforted" situation with its oxymoronic "beautiful poverty" and "sumptuous destitution." In his newly won independence he now pities the poor soul who, degrading himself, "goes to a shadow to beg alms." This is a repudiation of his "ode." Far from being a cause of discontent, his isolation and loneliness are precious to him because thereby he gains emotional and artistic freedom to create. "The shadow" of the poem is again Stalin. In this poem there are echoes of his youthful verse "The Pedestrian" (32). The "beggar-woman friend" is probably Natalya Shtempel, who had helped the exiled Mandelstam and saved most of his unpublished poems and letters.

7

For almost a quarter of a century after his death Mandelstam's name was consigned, by the official curators of Soviet letters, to oblivion. They almost succeeded. What could Mandelstam's lyrics possibly mean to new generations unfamiliar with Stalin's rule almost half a century ago? It is well known that, as the years recede, many politically inspired poems fade as distance blurs their image, freeze into immobility, and lose their special poignancy. Yet this was not the fate of Mandelstam's poetry because its anguished expression has not lost universal appeal, nor its cry for intellectual honesty ageless validity. Thus, despite all the efforts of the literary apparatchiks, this wonderful annalist of an era of transition and pain remained very much alive in the collective memory of poetry lovers in Russia. Time has served only to confirm his status as one of the few contemporary writers from whom sophisticated and skeptical readers alike will accept intellectual and spiritual nourishment; and his heritage, speaking a sorrowful yet visionary truth to two generations of Russians accustomed to introspection and meditation, has continued to shine as a heroic beacon of artistic freedom.

A few years ago, as a result of political changes, the Soviets came to an important crossroads in their turbulent history. They have been introducing a sense of democracy into their social and cultural life and initiating a series of extremely bold attempts to reshape their country in the crucible of contemporary reality. They have been encouraging a more open society and revealing some painful details about their past that have been previously concealed and denied. Preoccupation with a long-buried past, excavating passions as well as facts, an experiment involving immense political risks, has now become a powerful trend in Soviet life, although the battle for social and intellectual *perestroika* is still far from won because some hard-line bureaucrats and conservatives still insist on keeping the genie in the bottle, fearful that the new process will open up old wounds in Russia's social psyche. Whatever the deeper significance of these warming winds of openness, they represent a welcome change from decades of cultural stagnation when writers and artists had to conform to the suffocating tenets of social realism in order to gain official sanction. Like a breath of fresh air the new trend seems to blow away the cobwebs of neglect and indifference accumulated during the long tenure of literary philistines on the Soviet cultural scene, who made the poetry and prose of the period colorless, drab, and without enduring artistic value. Nothing is more exhilarating in the world today than the political, social and cultural rebound of the Soviet Union. Moscow and Leningrad will soon again be among the world centers of art and literature.

At the dawn of what promises to be a new era, the suppression of Mandelstam's work, as Garcia Lorca once said about the social art of the Spanish theater, may lead to a public tribunal where mistakes of the troubled past will be submitted as evidence and a few accidental survivors will furnish their testimony, to explain the eternal norms of human hearts and sentiments. Thus, in an extraordinary reversal, the dead poet may assume the role of public prosecutor bearing witness to certain universal moral ideals, and readers will be called upon to become a sort of historical jury to pronounce a verdict on the sins of the period. Hence, in this great politico-social turnover, Mandelstam might still score a posthumous victory. Poetic justice has its own quixotic way of triumphing over death and mending the ravages of insensitivity and barbarism.

While it is only fair to say that a great deal has still to be done after seventy years of systematic suppression of writers, artists, scientists, and philosophers and that skeptics may be justified in urging caution, it is difficult to deny any longer that something exciting and important—close to a cultural renaissance—is happening in today's Soviet Union as old taboos are broken, hundreds of formerly forbidden topics are openly argued, and new revelations are made every day. As a symbol of this changing climate and of the willingness of the authorities to revoke censorship and restraints on freedom of speech, literature, and the arts, Andrey Sakharov, the distinguished civil-rights leader, was called back from his exile, permitted to speak, write, travel abroad.

Unfortunately this physically frail and spiritually relentless man, the prickly conscience of the Soviet Union, with his consuming passion for peace and justice who courageously continued his struggle for a more humane society even after his election to the new Soviet Congress of People's Deputies, recently died. President Gorbachev mourned the national loss of "a man of conviction and sincerity."[67] *Doctor Zhivago* was finally published. Also published was Anna Akhmatova's powerful poem "Requiem," a single heart-rending cry for the victims of Stalin's terror. One of the most recent publications is Anatoly Rybakov's *Children of Arbat,* an unflinching look at the oppression by Stalin whom he accuses of plotting Kirov's murder, and its impact on the young generation. Rybakov is currently working on the sequel to the *Children of Arbat.* The silence is now over and the subject of Stalin's victims is at the heart of a national debate. The poem "Monument not yet erected" by Yevgeny Yevtushenko is a plea for a public memorial to the millions of innocent victims of Stalin's purges. Especially moving are the following lines of Yevtushenko's poem: "Monuments not yet erected unearth their tortured comrades / Free them with pickaxes, now frozen sculptures, from Siberian graves; / And then with woodman's gloves, near-frozen, almost marble, / Go rapping at all doors where they have been forgotten."[66] Even Solzhenitsyn's *One Day in the Life of Ivan Denisovich* was recently reissued and—wonder of wonders—his epic labor camp memoirs *The Gulag Archipelago,* which first documented the existence of a network of labor- and punitive camps in the Soviet Union and for which he was called an enemy of the Soviet State fourteen years ago, exiled from the country and stripped of his citizenship, will soon be published in the prestigious *Novy Mir* and his citizenship restored. And, finally, after the huge night and boundless darkness, the dizzying conclusion of the last decade—the harnessing of popular rage against the dictatorships for freedom, multiparty system, and open borders resulting in an incredibly fast democratization process in the countries of Eastern Europe best symbolized by the crumbling of the Berlin wall—marked the dramatic end of this historical period.

In this refreshing spirit of cultural *glasnost*, admirers of Mandelstam feel that there could hardly be a more apposite moment for the Soviet Writers' Union to publish a multivolume, definitive edition of his writings, with all the sociohistorical contextual annotation that such an edition deserves. Some of Mandelstam's poems may still be hidden somewhere in the Soviet Union and, as this *versunkenes Kulturgut* is being gradually unearthed, this new edition, filling the gap, should include such newly revealed writings as well, providing richer details of Mandelstam's artistry. It may help to unravel many of the poet's enigmas and may offer fresh interpretations as part of a vital, ongoing discussion of his immortal gifts. Mandelstam has never been more alive than today.

ERVIN C. BRODY

Notes

1. Albert Camus, *Resistance, Rebellion and Death* (New York: Vintage, 1974), 250, 268, 271.
2. Ronald Hingley, *Nightingale Fever* (New York: Knopf, 1981), 8.
3. Boris Pasternak, *Doctor Zhivago* (New York: Signet, 1958), 431.
4. Hingley, *Nightingale Fever*, 10.
5. This number and others in parentheses refer to numbers of poems included in this volume. When no number or only the indication of the year follows, the poem is not included.
6. Joseph Brodsky, introduction to *Osip Mandelstam 50 Poems*, trans. Bernard Meares (New York: Persea, 1977), 15.
7. Ibid., 14.
8. Osip Mandelstam, "Two Poems About Stalin," trans. by Herbert Marshall, in *Center for Soviet and East European Studies*, no. 30 (Carbondale: Southern Illinois University, 1984).
9. Ronald Hingley, *Pasternak, A Biography* (New York: Knopf, 1983), 119.
10. Hingley, *Nightingale Fever*, 10.
11. Isaiah Berlin, *Personal Impressions* (New York: Viking, 1980), 192.
12. Clarence Brown, *Mandelstam* (London: Cambridge University Press, 1973), 238.
13. Bernard Meares, in *Osip Mandelstam 50 Poems*, 21.
14. Christopher Lehmann-Haupt, "Nadezhda Mandelstam's *Hope Against Hope*," *New York Times*, 19 October 1970.
15. Gian Carlo Menotti, "I forgive Goethe, Tolstoy, and, above all, Mozart," *New York Times*, 10 June 1989.
16. Steven Broyde, *Osip Mandelstam and His Age* (Cambridge: Harvard University Press, 1975), 3.
17. Clarence Brown and W. S. Merwin, eds., *Selected Poems* (New York: Atheneum, 1974), ix.
18. Camus, *Lyrical and Critical Essays* (New York: Vintage, 1970), 13.
19. Nils Ake Nilsson, "Osip Mandelstam and His Poetry," in *Major Soviet Writers*, ed. Edward J. Brown (London, Oxford, New York: Oxford University Press, 1973), 165.
20. William Shakespeare, *Macbeth*, 2.3.52–56.
21. Mandelstam, *The Complete Critical Prose and Letters*, ed. Jane Gary Harris (Ann Arbor, Mich.: Ardis, 1979), 121.
22. Simon Leys, *The Burning Forest: Essays on Chinese Culture and Politics* (New York: Holt, Rinehart and Winston, 1985), 14.
23. Camus, *Exile and Kingdom* (New York: Vintage, 1958), 158.
24. Feodor Dostoevsky, *The Double* (Bloomington: Indiana University Press, 1958), 254.
25. *The Prose of Osip Mandelstam*, ed. Clarence Brown (Princeton: Princeton University Press, 1965), 37–41.
26. Dostoevsky, *Crime and Punishment* (New York: Norton, 1975), 8–13.

27. Brown and Merwin, *Selected Poems*, xi.

28. Broyde, *Mandelstam*, 201.

29. Ibid., 6.

30. Meares, in *Osip Mandelstam 50 Poems*, 15.

31. Hingley, *Nightingale Fever*, 75.

32. Pushkin, *Boris Godunov*, in *Nineteenth Century Russian Plays*, ed. F. D. Reeve (New York: Norton, 1973), 224–26, 175–76.

33. Anthony Austin, "For Moscow intellectuals the night is long and cold," *New York Times*, 30 October 1980.

34. Mandelstam, *Critical Prose and Letters*, 120.

35. Quoted in Donal Henahan, "The Everlasting Enigma of the 'Ring,'" *New York Times*, 6 November 1988.

36. Ibid.

37. *Prose of Mandelstam*, 102–3.

38. Ibid., 103.

39. Pasternak, *Doctor Zhivago*, 153–54.

40. Ibid., 155.

41. Ibid., 164.

42. Ibid., 165.

43. Ibid., 171.

44. Ibid., 202.

45. Ibid., 216.

46. Hingley, *Pasternak*, 207.

47. Ibid., 155.

48. *Prose of Mandelstam*, 76.

49. Ibid.

50. Ibid., 73–75.

51. Stanley Kunitz, "Soviet poets are heard in Philadelphia," *New York Times*, 21 March 1989.

52. *Prose of Mandelstam*, 120–21.

53. Ibid., 75, 79.

54. Brown, *Mandelstam*, 197.

55. Brodsky, in *Osip Mandelstam 50 Poems*, 10.

56. *Prose of Mandelstam*, 103.

57. Hingley, *Nightingale Fever*, 14.

58. Quoted in Walter Goodman, "Writers Discuss Theme of Myth in Modern Life," *New York Times*, 13 October 1984.

59. Edward J. Brown, *Major Soviet Writers*, 7–32.

60. Quoted in Henry Gifford, *Pasternak* (Cambridge: Cambridge University Press, 1977), 5.

61. Ibid.

62. *Bartlett's Familiar Quotations* (Boston, Toronto: Little, Brown, 1980), 538, 640.

63. *Selections from the Prose and Poetry of Pushkin*, ed. Ernest J. Simmons (New York: Dell, 1961), 65.

64. Mandelstam, *Critical Prose and Letters*, 475.

65. *Four Great Plays by Ibsen*, introduction by John Gassner (New York: Bantam, 1971), 215.

66. "Yevtushenko plea for Stalin victims," *Observer* (London), 10 January 1989.

67. *New York Times*, 16 December 1989.

Poems from Mandelstam

From *Stone*

2

With tinsel gold the Christmas trees
are shining brightly in the forests;
among the bushes the toy wolves
are staring with their fearsome eyes.

O sorrow, my prophetic sorrow,
O stillness of my silent freedom,
and ever-laughing crystal of
the lifeless canopy of heaven!

1908

4

To read only children's books,
to cherish only children's thoughts,
to disperse far everything large,
to rise out of profound sadness.

I am mortally tired of life,
I get nothing out of it,
but I love my poor land
because I've not seen any other.

I swung in a far-off garden
on a plain wooden swing,
and remember in misty delirium
the tall, dark spruces.

1908

5

Tenderer than tender
is your face,
whiter than white
your hand;
you are far away
from the whole world,

and everything yours
comes from the inevitable.

From the inevitable
your sadness
and the fingers of hands
that do not lose their warmth,
and the quiet sound
of undespondent speech,
and the far-awayness
of your eyes.

1909

6

On the pale blue of the enamel,
such as is thinkable in April,
the birches, lifting up their branches,
slipped imperceptibly towards evening.

A light design and finely finished,
the slender little net has hardened,
neatly delineated like
a drawing on a china plate,

when on the firmament of glass
the gracious artist sets it there
in consciousness of short-lived power,
oblivious of mournful death.

1909

7

There is a chaste sorcery:
lofty harmony, profound peace,
and the lares I have installed
far from ethereal lyres.

By their thoroughly-cleansed niches,
in the hours of attentive sunsets,
I listen to the ever-rapturous
silence of my penates.

What a toylike destiny, what
timid laws, the chiseled
torso and the cold of these
frail bodies command!

No need to glorify other gods:
they are as if one's equals,
and one is allowed with a careful hand
to set them in another place.

1909

8

This body given to me—what shall I do
with it, this thing so single, so much mine?

For the quiet joy of breathing and of living,
tell me, to whom have I to give my thanks?

I am the gardener, I am the flower too,
not lonely in the prison of the world.

My warmth, my breathing, has already lain
upon the glass panes of eternity.

On it will be imprinted a design
unrecognizable in recent times.

Let the moment's lees come flowing down—
the gracious pattern cannot be struck out.

1909

9

Sadness beyond expression
opened two enormous eyes,
the flower vase awoke
and splashed out its crystal.

The whole room was intoxicated
with lassitude—sweet medicine!
Such a little kingdom
had absorbed so much sleep.

A little red wine,
a little sunshiny May—
and the whiteness of slenderest fingers
breaking a thin biscuit.

1909

10

Drawing the silk threads
onto the mother-of-pearl
shuttle, O supple fingers,
begin your enchanting lesson!

The hands' tides are
monotonous motions;
without doubt you are
invoking some solar scare

when a hand's broad palm, like
a blazing shell, now dies out,
gravitating towards the shadows,
now goes off into rose-colored fire!

Date unknown

11

No need to talk of anything,
nothing has to be studied,
the dark, savage soul is both
sad like this and beautiful:

it doesn't want to study anything,
it is quite unable to talk
and swims like a young dolphin
through the gray abyss of the world.

1909

13

More sluggish is the snowy hive,
more limpid is the window's crystal,
and on the chair a turquoise veil
lies where it has been carelessly thrown.

The fabric, heady with itself,
and pampered by the light's caress,
feels it's experiencing summer,
as if it were not touched by winter;

and if, enclosed in icy diamonds,
there streams the frost of endless time,
here is the palpitation of
ephemeral, blue-eyed dragon-flies.

1910

14. Silentium

She has not yet been born,
she is both music and word,
and therefore the inviolable
bond of everything living.

The sea's breast is breathing calmly,
but, as if reckless, the day
is bright, and the foam's pale lilac
is in a dull-azure vessel.

May my lips find
primordial muteness,
like a crystalline note
that is pure from birth!

Remain foam, Aphrodite,
and, word, turn back into music,
and be ashamed, heart's heart
poured out from fundamental life!

1910

15

Hearing is straining its keen sail,
wide-eyed gazing is growing empty
and through the peacefulness there swims
the unloud choir of midnight birds.

I am as poor as nature is
and I am plain as are the skies,
and shadowy my freedom is,
like voices of the midnight birds.

I see the moon of lifelessness
and sky that's deathlier than canvas;
your world of strangeness and of pain
I take upon me, emptiness!

1910

17

I grew out of an evil, slimy pool,
rustling with a reed pen

and passionately, languidly, caressingly
breathing forbidden life.

And not noticed by anyone, I droop
into a cold and swampy refuge,
met by the welcoming rustling
of the short autumn minutes.

I am happy with this cruel insult
and, in life that is like a dream,
I secretly envy each person
and am secretly in love with each.

1910

19

Sultry twilight covers the bed,
my chest breathes with effort. . . .
Perhaps dearer to me than all else
are life's subtle cross and the secret way.

1910

20

How slowly the horses go, how little
light there is in the street lamps!
The strange people no doubt know
where they are taking me.

And I trust in their care,
I am cold, I want to sleep;
I was tossed up at the road's bend
to meet a star's ray.

The swaying of my burning head
and the tender ice of someone else's hand,

and the outlines of the dark spruces,
are still mysterious to me.

1911

22

The cloudy air is moist and resonant;
it's good in the forest and not frightening.
Again obediently I bear
the light cross of lonely walks.

And again like a wild duck my reproach
will fly up to an indifferent fatherland—
I take part in gloomy life
and I am guiltless in being lonely!

A shot rang out. Over the drowsy lake
the ducks' wings are heavy now,
and the pines' trunks are stupefied
by the reflected twofold existence.

The wan sky with its strange reflection
is the world's misty suffering—
O allow me too to be misty
and allow me to love you not.

1911

23

Today is a bad day,
the grasshoppers' choir sleeps
and grimmer than gravestones is
the gloom of the rocks' tent.

Ringing and flash of arrows
and prophetic crows' cry . . .
I'm dreaming a bad dream,
moment by moment flies.

Extend the verge of phenomena,
demolish this earthly cage,
and burst into fierce hymn,
rioting mysteries' copper!

O stern souls' pendulum,
it oscillates deaf, straight,
and passionately fate knocks
upon our forbidden door. . . .

1911

24

A black wind is rustling
the vaguely breathing leaves
and a fluttering swallow
draws a circle in dark sky.

In my tender, dying heart
incipient twilight
is quietly arguing
with a ray that is burning out.

And a copper moon has come out
above a forest sinking into evening.
Why so little music
and such tranquillity?

1911

26. The Shell

Perhaps you do not need me, night;
out of the abyss of the world,
like a shell without a pearl,
I was cast up on your shore.

Indifferent, you make waves foam,
you sing intractably; but you

will come to love and appraise
the falsehood of the useless shell.

You'll lie beside it on the sand
and clothe it with your chasuble;
you'll link with it inseparably
the huge bell of the sea-surge;

and the walls of the fragile shell,
like the house of an uninhabited heart,
you'll fill with whispers of the foam
and with the mist and wind and rain. . . .

1911

27

O heaven, heaven, I shall dream of you!
It cannot be that you should grow quite blind,
and day should be burnt up like a white page:
a little smoke and then a little ash!

1911

30

In the mist I could not feel your image,
agonizing and unstable shape.
"Lord!" I said, and by mistake I said it,
without thinking that was what I'd say.

The name of God, great as a great bird,
flew forth from my breast. Ahead of me
is the wreathing vapor of dense mist,
and the empty cage is left behind.

1912

31

No, not the moon, but a bright clock-face shines
at me, and how am I to blame in that
I feel the milkiness of strengthless stars?

I find the loftiness of Batyushkov
repugnant: "What's the time?" they asked him here;
"Eternity," he answered the curious ones.

1912

32. The Pedestrian

I feel an unconquerable fear
in the presence of mysterious heights,
I am content with a swallow in the skies
and I love the flight of bell-towers!

And, it seems, an ancient pedestrian
over the abyss, on a decaying footway
I hear how a ball of snow is growing
and eternity is beating on the stone hours.

If it were so! But I am not that traveler
who flashes for a moment on faded foliage;
and sadness sings authentically in me.

An avalanche indeed is in the mountains!
And all of my soul is in the bells,
but music from the chasm will not save us!

1912

41. The Old Man

It is already light, a Siren
is singing in the morning's
seventh hour. Old man resembling
Verlaine—now it is your time!

In his eyes is a green light,
either cunning or childlike;
round his neck is pinned
a patterned Turkish kerchief.

He blasphemes, mutters
incoherent words;
he wishes to make confession,
but first of all to sin.

A disappointed workman,
or a distressed spendthrift—
but his eye blackened in the depths
of night blooms like a rainbow.

Thus, observing the Sabbath
day, he plods along, when
out of every gateway
hilarious trouble peers;

and at home, with winged
abuse, pale with rage,
his stern wife meets
the drunken Socrates!

1913

47

In quiet suburbs yard-keepers
are shoveling up snow;
I am walking with bearded
muzhiks, a person passing by.

Women in kerchiefs appear briefly,
and crazy mongrels yap,
and the scarlet roses of samovars
burn in the taverns and houses.

1913

The Valkyries are flying, the bows sing.
The cumbrous opera is drawing to a close.
On the marble staircases, attendants
with heavy fur coats await the gentlefolk.

The curtain is ready to fall hermetically;
some fool is still clapping in the gods;
cabmen are dancing round their bonfires.
So-and-so's coach! Departure. The End.

1913

62

The orioles are in the woods, and length of vowels
within the tonic verses is the only measure.
But only once a year is there poured out in nature
the selfsame quantity as is in Homer's metrics.

As if that day were a caesura, it yawns wide:
from very morning, peace and arduous longueurs;
the oxen pasturing . . . Such golden indolence
as draws no richness of a whole note from a reed.

1914

65

Nature is that same Rome and is reflected in it.
We see images of Rome's civil might
in the transparent air, as in the blue Circus;
on the fields' Forum; and in the Colonnade of a grove.

Nature is that same Rome, and it seems that again
we have no need to trouble the gods in vain:
there are sacrifices' entrails, so that we may divine war;
slaves, that we may keep silence; and stones, that we may build!

1914

66

Let the names of flourishing cities
caress the ear with their fleeting importance.
Not Rome the city lives amid the ages,
but man's place in the universe.

Emperors strive to subdue him,
priests justify the wars,
but without man houses and altars,
like wretched trash, are worthy of contempt.

Date unknown

67

I have not heard the tales of Ossian,
I have not tasted age-old wine—
why then do I seem to see a field
and Scotland's murderous moon?

And in the sinister silence I seem to hear
the roll-call of the raven and the harp,
and, streaming in the wind, the scarves of men-at-arms
are glimpsed by the light of the moon.

I received a blissful inheritance:
the wandering dreams of foreign singers;
we are free to disdain deliberately
our kinship and tedious neighborhood.

And perhaps not one treasure alone will pass
grandchildren by and go on to great-grandchildren,
and again a skald will compose a foreign song
and will utter it as his own.

1914

69. The Staff

My staff, my freedom,
core of my existence—
will my truth soon become
the truth of the people?

I did not bow to the earth
before I had found myself;
I took my staff, became enlivened
and went to distant Rome.

Though the snows may never thaw
on the black plow-lands,
still the sadness of my people at home
is foreign to me as before.

The snow on the rocks will thaw,
scorched by the sun of truth.
The people were right, entrusting
the staff to me, who have seen Rome!

1914

73

A flame is destroying
my dry life, and now
I sing not of stone,
but of wood.

It is light and rugged;
of one piece are
the heart of the oak
and the fisherman's oars.

Drive the piles in harder,
hammer away, hammers,
about wooden Paradise
where things are so light.

1914

76

From Tuesday until Saturday
only a wilderness spread out.
O how protracted these migrations!
Five thousand miles a single arrow.

And when the swallows flew to Egypt
across the waters of their way,
for four days they were hanging there,
ladling no water with a wing.

1915

From *Tristia*

In the various voices of a maidens' choir
all tender churches sing with their own voice,
and in stone arches of the Cathedral of the Assumption
I seem to see arched eyebrows, high above.

And from a rampart fortified by archangels
I viewed a city on a marvelous height.
Inside the Acropolis's walls I was consumed
by sorrow for the Russian name and Russian beauty.

And was it not amazing that we should dream of an orchard
where pigeons were soaring in the ardent blue;
that a nun should be singing neumes of Orthodox chants:
an Assumption with the tenderness of Florence in Moscow?

And the five-domed cathedrals of Moscow
with their Italian and their Russian soul
remind me of the apparition of Aurora,
but with a Russian name, and in a fur coat.

1916

88

I'm feeling cold. Transparent springtime is
clothing Petropolis in a green down.
But still the Neva's wave, like a medusa,
inspires in me a slight sense of aversion.
On the embankment of the northern river
the fireflies of the automobiles whirl,
steel dragon-flies and beetles rush along,
the gold pins of the stars are flickering,
but no stars, no stars whatever, will kill
the weighty emerald of the sea's wave.

1916

In transparent Petropolis we'll die,
where we are in the power of Proserpine.
With every breath we drink in mortal air,
and every hour to us is mortal time.
Severe Athena, goddess of the sea,
take off your mighty helmet made of stone.
In transparent Petropolis we'll die,
where Proserpine, not you, reigns over us.

1916

103. The Twilight of Freedom

Brothers, let us glorify freedom's twilight,
the great twilight year.
Into the seething waters of night
a massive forest of snares is sunk.
Into unhearing years, O sun,
you are rising, judge and people.

And let us glorify the fateful
burden which in tears the nation's leader shoulders.
And glorify the somber burden of power,
its insupportable weighing-down.
In whom there is a heart—he must hear, time,
how your ship goes to the bottom.

We have bound the swallows together
in battle legions, and behold,
no sun is seen; the whole element
is twittering and moving, living;
through meshes of the dense twilight
no sun is seen, and the earth drifts.

But what, then, let us make the attempt: a huge and lumbering
and creaking turning of the rudder.
The world is drifting. Courage, men!
Parting the ocean as with a plow,
we shall remember even in Lethean frost
that the cost of the earth to us was ten heavens.

May 1918, Moscow

106

What steepness there is in the crystal pool!
The Sienese mountains intercede for us,
and the prickly cathedrals of insane cliffs
are hanging in midair, where wool and silence are.

From a suspended stairway of the prophets and kings
are let down an organ, fortress of the Holy Spirit,
the sheep-dogs' cheerful barking and good-natured fierceness,
the shepherds' sheepskins and the judges' staves.

Here is a fixed land and together with it
I drink the cold mountain air of Christianity,
the austere Credo and psalmodist's repose,
the keys and tatters of the apostolic churches.

What line could reproduce the crystal
of high notes in the fortified ether?—
and from Christian mountains in astonished space,
like a song of Palestine, God's benefaction descends.

1919

113

I cannot call to mind the word I wished to say.
The blind swallow will home into the hall of shadows,
on its clipped wings, to play with the translucent ones.
Unconsciously the night song will be sung.

No birds are heard. No everlastings flower.
Translucent are the manes of night's horse-herd.
On the dry river floats the empty skiff.
Among the grasshoppers the word becomes unconscious.

And slowly does it grow, as if a tent or shrine,
now it pretends to be insane Antigone,
now throws itself, a lifeless swallow, at our feet
with Stygian tenderness and with a twig of greenness.

O if one brought back too the shame of sighted fingers,
and all the salient joy of recognition.

I so much fear the sobs of Aonides,
the mist, the ringing and the yawning pit.

Mortals are given power to love and recognize,
for them sound too spills into fingers,
but what I wished to say, I have forgotten,
and bodiless thought will home into the hall of shadows.

This is not what the limpid one repeats,
always the swallow, friend, Antigone . . .
but on her lips, like some black ice there burns
the recollection of a Stygian sound.

November 1920

116

Take, for the sake of gladness, from my palms
a little sunlight and a little honey,
as Persephone's bees commanded us.

The boat not fastened cannot be untied,
the shadow shod in furs cannot be heard,
within dense life, fear can't be overcome.

Kisses remain for us, and nothing else,
covered in hairs, just like the little bees
that die when they have flown out of the hive.

They rustle in the night's transparent thickets,
their homeland's the dense forest of Taygetus,
their nutriment is time, lungwort and mint.

Take, for the sake of gladness, my wild present,
this dry and this uncomely-looking necklace
of dead bees and honey they've turned to sun.

November 1920

117

There the ciborium, like a golden sun,
has been hung in the air—this is the splendid moment;
no language but the Greek must ring out here: to take
into its hands the whole world, like a plain apple.

It is the solemn zenith of divine service,
light in a round temple under a dome in July,
that we, outside of time, with our full breast
should sigh for that meadow where time does not fly.

And like eternal noon the Eucharist lingers on:
all take the sacrament, all play and all sing,
and there, within the sight of all, the divine chalice
is streaming with an inexhaustible joyfulness.

Date unknown

From *Poems* 1928

134. Moscow Rain

. . . It gives, ever so scantily,
its sparrowy cold, a little to us,
a little to the tree-clumps, a little
to the cherries on the fruit-stand.

And in the darkness a seething grows,
a light bustling of tea-leaves,
as if an aerial ants'-nest
were feasting in the dark verdure;

from the fresh drops, a vineyard
has begun to stir in the grass.
It's as though a seed-bed of coldness
had opened in web-footed Moscow.

1922

139

Like a little corpuscle, with the brimming
sun's aid the incendiary sliver of glass
turned itself over with a pinion
and caught fire in the empyrean.

A mosquitolike trifle, the splinter
whimpered and tinkled at its zenith
and, under the carabids' muted
singing, agonized in the azure:

Don't forget me, put me to death,
but give me a name, give me a name!
I'll feel easier with it—catch me,
in the pregnant deep blue.

1923

142

You houses not high, with your little square windows,—
hello, hello, Petersburg's unsevere winter.

And the unfrozen skating-rinks stick out like pikes with their
     ribs,
and ice skates are still lying about in sightless vestibules.

And how long since the potter steered along the canal with his
     red earthenware,
selling his honest goods from the little granite steps?

They're wearing gumboots, they're wearing gray ones in the
     bazaar,
and the rind is peeling itself off the mandarins.

And roasted coffee in a bag—home straight from the cold,
the golden mocha ground in the electric coffee-mill.

Chocolate ones, brick ones, houses not high,
hello, hello, Petersburg's unsevere winter.

And waiting-rooms with grand pianos where, offering seats in
     armchairs,
doctors regale someone with heaps of old copies of *The Cornfield*.

After a bath, after the opera, it's all the same wherever you go.
The muddle-headed streetcar is warm.

1925

From Uncollected Poems

145

My silent dream, my every minute's dream:
a forest, spellbound and invisible,
where some vague kind of rustle is drifting,
like the miraculous rustling of silk curtains.

In misty meetings and insane debates,
at crossroads of astonished eyes the rustle,
invisible, incomprehensible,
like ashes blazed and is already out.

And as the mistiness clothes faces,
and a word dies faintingly upon the lips,
it seems too that a frightened bird has rushed
among the shrubs declining towards evening.

1908

146

Here toads that fill one with disgust
are jumping into the thick grass.
If death were not, then never should
I be aware that I am living.

And what do you two care for me,
life on the earth and beauty?—
But beauty has managed to remind me
who I am and who is my dream.

1909

147

A subtle decay grows thin.
A violet Gobelin.

The sky sinks towards us
onto water and forests.

An indecisive hand
portrayed these clouds,

and a sad gaze meets
their design covered with fog.

Dissatisfied and silent I stand—
I, the creator of my worlds,

where skies are artificial
and crystal dew sleeps.

1909

148

Below thunderclouds there floats
the scream of birds of prey:
enough fiery pages have already
been turned by the centuries.

Creatures live in sacred dread
and, like a swallow before the storm,
each will accomplish with its soul
its indescribable flight.

When will the sun melt you,
silver clouds, and will
the height be easy,
and will a calm spread its wings?

Date unknown

149

Where noisy glass tears
itself out of the torrent's
captivity, the swirling foam
cools like a swan's wing.

O time, do not torment with envy
him who has set in time.
Chance raised us up as foam
and put us together as lace.

Date unknown

150

Upon the altar of the hazy ripples
the mild god of the seas makes sacrifice.

The sea is indistinct, seething like wine;
the sun above it quivers like an eagle.

And nothing but the sea-mist's floating there,
and silence's resounding timbrel's heard,

and only heaven with its bright blue heart
adopts the sea's white haziness as its son.

And wider is the ocean when it sleeps,
and more restrained is its majestic roar.

And in the heavens, weighty and triumphal:
the semblance of an eagle cast in metal.

Date unknown

155

The new moon in the azure
is clear and it is high.
Horseshoes are testing
the roads' loud ground.

I took a deep breath,
as though I were scooping
with a silver ladle
in the blue sky.

I have put on good
fortune's weighty wreath;
in the cheerful forge
the blacksmith is at work.

1911

156

I am able to liberate my soul
from external conditions,
I hear my blood's singing and seething
and quickly grow tipsy.

And somewhere on the border
of languor, the primordial ringings
of substance native to me
again combine in a chain.

Our essences are weighed there
in the impartial ether:
starry weights are thrown
onto the trembling scales.

And in the limit's exultation
lies the rapture of life,
the body's recollection
of its unchangeable homeland.

1911

157

Spring's caress murmured,
a thousand-waved torrent.
A carriage glided, flashed past,
light as a butterfly.

I smiled at the spring,
I looked back stealthily:

a woman with sleek glove
was driving—just like a dream!

Off she went on her way,
dressed in silk mourning,
and her delicate veil
also was black. . . .

1911

159. The Barrel Organ

The barrel organ—plaintive singing,
the trash of leisurely arias—
like an ugly apparition
troubles the autumn canopy.

Clothe the sentimental emotion
in misty music, that this song
might for a moment stir
the laziness of stagnant water.

What an ordinary day! How impossible
is inspiration!—a needle in my
brain, I roam like a shadow.

I'd welcome the knife-grinder's
flint as a deliverance.
A vagabond, I love movement.

June 1912

162

Like a serpent, I am hidden
in myself; twining round myself
like ivy, I rise above myself;

I want myself, I fly to myself,
with dark wings extended
I flutter over the water;

and like a startled eagle
that returns and no longer finds its nest,
which has fallen into the abyss,

I will bathe myself in lightning's fire
and, cursing the grievous thunder,
will vanish in the cold cloud!

[*1912*]

163

The rabble slept. The square gapes in an arch.
The moonlight has been spilt on the bronze door.
Here Harlequin once sighed for brilliant glory,
and here a beast killed Alexander.

Pealing of chimes, and shades of former sovereigns . . .
Russia, you stand on stone, you stand on blood;
give me your blessing that, though through a burden,
I may take part in your last punishment!

1913

164. Self-Portrait

In the lifting of the head is a winged
allusion. But the suit is baggy.
In the eyes' closing, in the hands' repose,
is an untouched hiding-place of movement.

So this is he who has flight and song
and the ardent malleability
of the word, that with inborn rhythm
he may conquer his innate awkwardness.

1913

175

You went by through a cloud of mist.
Delicate rouge was on your cheeks.
The sun shines cold and ailing.
I wander free and useless. . . .
Malicious autumn tells fortunes over us,
threatens through ripe fruits,
speaks through summits from a summit
and kisses our eyes through gossamer.
How the dance of anxious life has stiffened
with cold! How your high color plays on
everything! How the gaping wound of bright days
shows through, even in the cloud of mist!

[*1914*]

178

Like sheep, in a pitiful mob
Euripides' elders hurried.
I go by the serpent's path
and in my heart is dark resentment.

But the hour is surely not far
when I shall shake off my sorrows,
as in the evening a boy
shakes the sand out of his sandals.

1914

182

Inconsolable words . . .
Judaea turned to stone,
and growing heavy with each moment,
His head drooped.
The soldiers stood guard
round the body growing cold.
Like a corolla, His head hung

on a slender and alien stem
and He reigned and bent
like a lily into its native pool,
and the depths where stems sink
celebrated their faith.

1915

183

Light vapor was melting away in the frosty air
and, oppressed by the sadness of freedom,
I'd have liked to be lifted up in a cold, quiet hymn,
to disappear for ever, but I was fated to go along
the snow-covered street in this evening hour. A dog's
barking was heard, and the sunset was not extinguished,
and I came across passers-by heading my way.
Don't talk to me! What will I answer you?

1915

184

The indignation of a senile cithara . . .
Rome's injustice is still alive,
and the dogs are howling, and the poor Tatars
in the remote villages of stony Crimea. . . .

O Caesar, Caesar! Do you hear the bleating
of flocks of sheep, and the motion of uneasy waves?
Why in vain do you pour out your radiance,
moon, a pitiful appearance without Rome?

You are not the one that in the night
gazes at the Capitol and lights up a forest
of cold pillars, but a village moon—
no more—a moon beloved of the hungry dogs!

October 1915

223

Succor me, O Lord, to live through this night:
I fear for my life, for Your handmaid—
to live in Petersburg's like sleeping in a coffin.

January 1931

273

Tatars, Uzbeks and Nenetses
and the whole Ukrainian people
and even the Germans on the Volga
are waiting for their translators.

And perhaps at this moment
some Japanese is translating me
into the Turkish language
and has penetrated into my very soul.

Date unknown

287

As from a single crack high in the mountains
flows water with a contradictory taste,
water half-hard, half-sweet, and double-faced,

so, in reality to die, do I
a thousand times a day forfeit my usual
freedom of breath and consciousness of goal.

December 1933, Moscow

292

To A. Bely

Caucasian mountains cried aloud to him,
and the crowded multitude of tender Alps;
on the steep upslopes of the sounding masses
his seeing foot set out upon its way.

And he, as only the mighty could, suffered
the ramification of European thought:
Rachel looked into the mirror of phenomena,
and Leah sang and her hands twined a wreath.

January 1934, Moscow

306

Yes, I am lying in the earth, moving my lips,
but every schoolboy will learn my words by heart:

roundest of all earth is the earth of the Red Square
and the voluntary declivity of the Square is solidifying,

the earth of the Red Square is roundest of all earth,
and the declivity of the Square is unexpectedly free,

it is being folded back down to the rice-fields,
so long as one last slave is living upon the earth.

May 1935, Voronezh

319

The wave runs, breaking the next wave's spine with a wave,
flinging itself upon the moon in slavish yearning;
the water's youthful Janizarian deep,
the unlulled capital city of the waves,
writhes, throws itself about and digs a moat in sand.

And through the gloomy and the cottony air
there seem to be the merlons of a wall still unbegun,

and down from foamy ladders fall the spattered
and separated soldiers of mistrustful sultans;
and the cold eunuchs carry round the poison.

July 1935, Voronezh

336

In my perception winter
is a belated gift:
I love, at the start,
its uncertain sweep.

As an alarm, it is beautiful,
like the beginning of stern deeds:
before the whole treeless cycle
even the raven's grown timid.

But precariously strongest of all
is the blue: the semicircular
temple-bone ice of salient
rivulets speaking without sleep. . . .

20–30 December 1936, Voronezh

341

Mounds of human heads recede into the distance,
I am diminishing there—already I'll not be noticed;
but in warm-hearted books and in children's games
I'll rise from the dead to say that the sun is shining.

[1936–37?]

350

What are we to do with the plains' beatenness,
with their miracle's drawn-out hunger?

Is not the openness we think in them
beheld by *us*, seen, as we fall asleep?
And ever the question grows: Whither and whence are they?
And does there not across them slowly creep
he about whom we cry out in our sleep,
the Judas of the future peoples?

16 January 1937, Voronezh

352

Don't make comparisons: what lives
is beyond compare. With what tender fright
I agreed with the equality of plains,
and the sky's circle was an ailment to me.

I appealed to the air-servant,
awaited service or news from it,
prepared for a journey, and floated
along an arc of unstarted voyages.

Where there is more sky for me, there I'm ready
to wander, and clear melancholy does not let me go
from the still young Voronezh hills
to those more human growing bright in Tuscany.

18 January 1937, Voronezh

354

Still I have not yet died, still I am not
alone, while, with my beggar-woman friend,
I find enjoyment in the grandeur of the plains,
and haze, and hunger, and the snowstorm.

In beautiful poverty, in sumptuous destitution
I live alone, serene and comforted; blessed
those days and blessed are those nights
and sinless the mellifluous labor.

Unfortunate is he whom barking scares
and whom the wind mows, like his shadow,
and poor is he who, more dead than alive,
goes to a shadow to beg alms.

January 1937, Voronezh

366

Breaches of rounded bays, and gravel, and the blue,
and the slow sail that is continued by a cloud—
I am cut off from you, your value scarcely told:
longer than organ fugues, the false-haired seaweed
is filled with a bitterness, and reeks of the long lie.
One's head grows tipsy with an iron tenderness,
and rust is gnawing a little at the sloping shore. . . .
What is this other sand that's laid beneath my head?
You are the guttural Urals, broad-shouldered Volga land
or this flat countryside—all my entitlements—
and with my whole breast I'm yet forced to breathe them in.

8 February 1937, Voronezh

374

I saw a lake, and it was standing sheer.
Fish, having built a house of freshness there,
were playing with a sliced rose in a wheel.
A fox and lion were struggling in a skiff.

Inside three barking portals there were staring
ills, foes of other still unopened arcs.
Across a violet span a gazelle went running,
and suddenly the rock there breathed as towers.

And honest sandstone, drunk with moisture, rose,
and in the midst of the artisan town-cricket
the urchin-ocean rose out of a river's freshness
and hurled cups of water into the clouds.

4–7 March 1937, Voronezh

From Uncollected Poems 1909–10?

457 (ii)

There is no other road
like that through your hand—
how else might I find
the land dear to me?

If you wish to help us sail
to those precious shores,
bring your hand close to your lips,
do not take it away.

The slender fingers tremble,
the frail body lives:
a boat gliding above
the water's moveless abyss.

[*1909*]

457 (iv)

At whom are you smiling,
O cheerful traveler!
Why do you bless
dales unknown to you?

No one is leading you
through valleys turning green,
and no one will call you
with the nightingale's murmur

when, wrapped in your cloak
that does not warm, but is dear to you,
you take flight along a humble ray
to the commanding stars.

[*1909–10?*]

457 (v)

In the twilight hall's spaciousness
is a respectful quiet.
As if in expectation of wine,
the empty crystal glasses surge,

their lips, blood-stained
in light-beams, stretching
hopelessly, tenderly opened
on the chaste stems.

Just look: we are intoxicated
with the unpoured wine.
What can be weaker than lilies
and sweeter than stillness?

[1909–10?]

457 (vi)

How autumn dies away in the
cold modulations of lyres!
How sweet and how unbearable
is its golden-stringed clergy!

Autumn sings in church choirs
and in monastery evenings
and, scattering ashes into urns,
seals wine into amphoras.

Like a calmed vessel with an
already settled liquid,
the spiritual is accessible to the gaze,
and its outlines are alive.

[1909–10?]

457 (ix)

Do not speak to me of eternity—
I am unable to contain it. But
how could one not forgive the eternity
of my love, of my lack of cares?

I hear how it grows and rolls
in a midnight billow.
But whoever approaches too
close pays too dearly.

And from a distance I am glad
of the quiet echo of its noise—
of its foaming masses—thinking
of what is dear and insignificant.

[1909–10?]

457 (xii)

If the winter morning
is dark, your cold window
looks like an old panel.

The ivy in front of the window
shows green; and below the icy glass
stand quiet trees under their cover,

protected from all winds,
guarded from every misfortune
and with branches interlaced.

The half-light is growing radiant.
Before the very window-frame
a silky last leaf shivers.

[1909–10?]

457 (xiii)

Your place is empty. The wind
keeps on, oppressed by your
absence. The drink destined for you
is steaming on the table.

So you will not approach with
the divining footsteps of a hermit;
and with sleepy lips you will not
trace a design on the glass;

in vain the long-suffering drink—
while it's still steaming—
draws playful sinuosities
in the deserted air.

[*1909–10?*]

457 (xiv)

The autumn Pleiades have caught
fire in the humble, wise heights.
And there is no delight whatever,
and no bitterness, in the worlds.

In everything there are monotonous
sense and complete freedom:
does nature not embody
the harmony of superior numbers?

But snow has fallen, and the trees'
nakedness has become funereal;
in the evening the golden emptiness
of the skies has opened in vain;

and the white, the black, the golden—
saddest of consonances—
have been called away
by imminent and final winter.

[*1909–10?*]

457 (xv)

Prophetic breath of my
verses' life-giving spirit,
what hearts do you touch,
what hearing do you reach?

Or are you more deserted by melody
than those shells singing in the sand,
whose sphere of beauty, outlined to them,
they did not open for the living?

[1909–10?]

457 (xvi)

Henceforth it is given
to my heart as its sole
delight—fall untiringly,
secret fountain.

In high sheaves, fly up
and tumble down and with
all your voices suddenly
at once become silent.

But clothe all my soul
in a chasuble of significant
thought, like the trembling
canopy of a moist larch.

[1909–10?]

457 (xvii)

When the bells' reproach pours
from the ancient church-towers,
and the very air is ill with the din,
and there are neither prayers nor words,

I am crushed, deadened. Wine,
and more strongly, more painfully,
has touched my heart's intoxication,
and again I am unassuaged.

I do not want my holy things,
I will break my vows—
and incomprehensible wormwood
overfills my soul.

[*1909–10?*]

457 (xix)

I see a stone sky over
the water's dull web.
My soul lives wearisomely
in the grip of hateful Erebus.

I understand this horror
and comprehend this tie:
and the sky falls without breaking,
and the sea splashes without foaming.

O chimera's pale wings
on the sand's rough gold,
and sail's gray trefoil,
like my yearning, crucified!

[*1909–10?*]

From Supplementary Uncollected Poems
1908–37

497

The music of your footsteps
in the forest snow's silence;

and, like a lingering shadow,
you descended into frosty day.

The winter is deep as night.
The snow hangs like a fringe.

The raven on its bough
has seen a lot in its time.

And the rising wave
of surging sleep

inspiredly shatters
the young, thin ice,

the thin ice of my soul
ripening in the silence.

[*1908–9*]

499

Enough of this slyness: I know
that I am fated to die;
and I am hiding nothing,
I can have no secrets from the Muse. . . .

And strangely, the knowledge is pleasant,
that I'll not know how to breathe;
it is a misty enchantment
and a sacrament, to die. . . .

I drowsily rock in a haze
and wisely remain silent:
my coming eternity
is irrevocably decided!

[*1908 or 1911*]

503

I am used to my heart's divining
the leaves' sympathetic rustle,
I read in the obscure patterns
the language of a humble heart.

True, clear thoughts
are a transparent, precise fabric. . . .
The keen leaves calculated—
stop playing with words.

Your leafy murmur goes
to the heights of some gleam:
the dark tree of the word,
the thoughts' tree that went blind?

May 1910, Helsingfors

511

In a white Paradise lies the epic hero:
plowman of war, aged peasant.
The world's expanse is in his gray eyes:
the dominating face of the Great Russian.

Only the saints can lie like this
in a fragrant grave, freeing
their hands in a sign of bliss
to savor their glory and their repose.

Is Russia not really a white Paradise
and are our dreams not joyful ones?
Rejoice, warrior, and do not die:
grandchildren and great-grandchildren have been saved.

December 1914

Notes

The numbers introducing the notes are poem numbers.

2. The first stanza only of this poem, one of Mandelstam's earliest, was published in the 1916 edition of *Stone* and is an example of his at times extreme brevity. The second stanza, restored in the same book's 1923 edition, markedly and subtly extends the poem's perspective. (Like most of Mandelstam's other poems, this one has no title.)

31. *Batyushkov.* Pushkin's elder contemporary and exemplar, the poet Konstantin Nikolayevich Batyushkov (1787–1855). We know from other writings of Mandelstam how greatly he admired Batyushkov.

73. Mandelstam here sings in praise of *wood*, in contradistinction to the *stone* from which this book takes its title.

84. *Neumes.* Signs used in early music to indicate the structure of a melody; forerunners of present-day notation.

88. *Petropolis* (Greek for Petersburg). Used by a number of Russian authors as an alternative name for Saint Petersburg-Petrograd-Leningrad. It was specially favored by Mandelstam.

89. Proserpine-Persephone, the wife of Hades, and the formidable queen of the Shades, rules over the souls of the dead. She displaces Minerva-Athena, goddess of wisdom and preserver of the state, who presides over the intellectual and moral side of human life. This famous poem of 1916 was written during the Great War as Petersburg moved rapidly and ominously toward the food riots and revolutions of 1917.

103. One of Mandelstam's most powerful poems of the period of the revolution, World War I, and civil war, *The Twilight of Freedom* contains a striking example of the poet's swallow imagery—symbolizing lightness, the soul, the human spirit—set here in the somber and menacing historical context.

106. The poem gives the impression of roving over the real or imagined canvas of a painting by an Italian master of the Sienese school, until the poet breathes the very air of the Christian tradition that inspired it.

113. *Aonides.* The Muses.

116. *Taygetus.* A lofty range of mountains separating Laconia and Messenia and extending from the frontiers of Arcadia down to the promontory of Taenarum. No necessary link with Persephone is apparent.

142. *The Cornfield.* A Russian weekly illustrated family magazine published in Saint Petersburg from 1870 to 1918.

163. *Alexander.* After several assassination attempts, Tsar Alexander II was fatally injured by a bomb thrown at him by I. I. Grinyevitsky near his Saint Petersburg palace in March 1881. In the following month the Tsar's five assassins, including one woman, were publicly hanged.

287. These six lines, formerly published as an original poem of Mandelstam,

were found to be a variant of the sestet of his translation of Petrarch's sonnet beginning: "Or che 'l ciel e la terra e 'l vento tace."

292. *To A. Bely.* One of a cycle of poems written in memory of Andrey Bely (pseudonym of Boris Nikolayevich Bugayev, 1880–1934). Bely, Symbolist poet and novelist and one of the leading literary figures of the time, in 1912 came under the influence of Rudolf Steiner (1861–1925), the Austrian theosophist and later founder of anthroposophy.

319. *Janizarian.* Much of Mandelstam's imagery is linked with his constant vision across the ocean of European and Eastern history. The Janizaries, members of the Turkish infantry, were the sultan's guards and main fighting force of the army. In the sixteenth century the Turks levied a tribute of Christian children (hence "youthful"?) whose prolonged and severe military training produced troops (the Janizaries and Spahis) unrivaled in loyalty and fanaticism.

341. Into this single quatrain, which might well serve as his epitaph, is compressed much of the quintessential Mandelstam: profound insight into the pity and terror of Russian history in his time and an inescapable foreboding that he was a doomed being, together with tenderness, love, and belief in a better future.

350. Is this an apocalyptic vision in which the plains, and we ourselves, are open not so much to a Second Coming as to a Second Betrayal? To Mandelstam in exile in Voronezh in 1937, Judas must often have seemed close at hand. Nadezhda Mandelstam's comments in *Hope Against Hope* (1970) on the Voronezh poems of this period suggest that Judas here represents Stalin.

374. Thanks to the researches of Clarence Brown, we know that this striking poem is based on the design of a stained-glass window and other architectural features of Notre-Dame, Paris.

457. To prevent alphabetical confusion, Roman numerals (ii–xix) replace Russian letters in the numbering of this sequence.

Index of First Lines